GUIDE TO COVERAGE OF COMMUNITIES OF WRITERS AND READERS

If you go to college, hold a job, and join a civic group, you're participating right now in the broad academic, work, and public communities.

ACADEMIC COMMUNITY	WORK COMMUNITY	PUBLIC COMMUNITY
Students, teachers, and others create and exchange knowledge through research, analysis, and interpretation.	Co-workers, managers, clients, and others exchange information, solve problems, and promote an organization.	Residents, leaders, volunteers, and others support a cause, supply information, or partici- pate in civic exchanges.

As you talk, read, and write in a community, you'll learn to recognize different community expectations—what readers want or need—and to tailor your choices as a writer to meet those expectations.

STRATEGIES FOR WRITING AND READING IN COMMUNITIES

TIPS FOR WRITING AND READING IN COMMUNITIES

THE
Longman Pocket Writer's Companion

CHRIS M. ANSON
North Carolina State University

ROBERT A. SCHWEGLER
University of Rhode Island

MARCIA F. MUTH
University of Colorado at Denver

Longman

New York San Francisco Boston
London Toronto Sydney Tokyo Singapore Madrid
Mexico City Munich Paris Cape Town Hong Kong Montreal

Senior Vice President and Publisher: Joseph Opiela
Acquisitions Editor: Susan Kunchandy
Supplements Editor: Donna Campion
Marketing Manager: Christopher Bennem
Senior Production Manager: Bob Ginsberg
Project Coordination, Text Design, and
    Electronic Page Makeup: Nesbitt Graphics, Inc.
Cover Design Manager and Cover Designer: John Callahan
Manufacturing Buyer: Lucy Hebard
Printer and Binder: R. R. Donnelley & Sons Company
Cover Printer: Coral Graphic Services, Inc.

For permission to use copyrighted material, grateful acknowledgment is made to
the copyright holders on pp. vi and 225-R, which are hereby made part of this
copyright page.

Library of Congress Cataloging-in-Publication Data

The Longman pocket writer's companion / Chris M. Anson, Robert A.
Schwegler, Marcia F. Muth.
    p. cm.
  Includes index.
  ISBN 0-321-08391-1
  1. English language—Rhetoric—Handbooks, manuals, etc. 2. Report
writing—Handbooks, manuals, etc. I. Title: Pocket writer's companion. II.
Anson, Christopher M., 1954- III. Schwegler, Robert A. IV. Muth, Marcia F.

PE1408 .L67 2003
808'.042—dc21   2002072480

Copyright © 2003 by Addison-Wesley Educational Publishers Inc.

Please visit our website at http://www.ablongman.com/anson

ISBN 0-321-08391-1

2345678910—DOC—050403

GUIDE FOR USING THIS HANDBOOK

When you're a busy writer in academic, work, and public communities, you want to make the most of your time. This book is designed to help you find what you need quickly and efficiently.

Strategy 1: Try the index at the end of the book. It includes key terms, subtopics, and related entries.

Strategy 2: Use the menu inside the front cover. This menu identifies sections and chapters so you can easily find main topics.

Strategy 3: Use the table of contents inside the back cover. Skim the contents to track down the chapter or topic you need. The chapter numbers and section letters noted there are used in cross-references and are easy to spot on the tabs on each page.

Strategy 4: Match editing symbols on your paper with corresponding sections of the text. The fold-in page on the back cover lists common revising and editing symbols. Identify the marks on your paper, and turn to the relevant section of the text.

Strategy 5: Check the Resources for Editing and the Glossary. Refer to useful grammar charts, or look up terms and usage questions in the Glossary.

Strategy 6: Use the special features of the text.
- **Look for the "read, recognize, and revise" approach.** Many chapters, especially those on grammar and usage, first introduce a problem using a Reader's Reaction and sample sentences. Then the chapter shows how to recognize and revise or edit the problem in your writing.

- **Use Read, Recognize, and Revise Ten Serious Errors.** Turn to this guide on p. 265. Look for a sentence like yours, and turn to the section noted for advice about how to recognize and remedy the problem.
- **Apply the Strategies.** Each Strategy suggests how to apply general advice, recognize problems, or revise and edit your own writing.
- **Compare the examples with your own sentences.** Skim the draft sentences in the section that seems the most likely place to look for a problem. Find a sentence like your own. Read the explanation with the example, and note any label so that you can learn how to recognize the problem. Use the revised or edited sentence as a pattern for your own changes.
- **Look for boldfaced terms.** These key terms are explained right in the text.
- **Find the ESL Advice.** If you are not a native speaker of English, look for the ESL Advice integrated in the text and in the Resources section at the back.
- **Look for charts and checklists.** Boxes help make useful information easy to spot.
- **Turn to sample documents.** Selections from two sample research papers (using the MLA and APA styles) show how other students have presented their papers. Sample documents in Chapter 6 also show how you might design a paper, letter, résumé, or poster.

Credits

Claude F. Boutron et al., "Decrease in Anthropogenic Lead, Cadmium, and Zinc in Greenland Snows since the Late 1960's," *Nature,* Vol. 353, 1991. **Michael Bright,** *Animal Language* (Ithaca, NY: Cornell University Press, 1984). *The Chicago Manual of Style* (14th ed., Chicago: The University of Chicago Press, 1993), p. 158. **Committee of Concerned Journalists,** "A Statement of Concern," *The Media & Morality,* edited by Robert M. Baird, William E. Loges, and Stuart E. Rosenbaum (New York: Prometheus Books, 1999). **Judith A. Cramer,** "Radio: A Woman's Place Is on the Air," *Women in Mass Communication* edited by Pamela J. Creedon (Woodland Hills, CA: Sage Publications, 1993). **Robert Daseler,** *Levering Avenue* Poems (Evansville: The University of Evansville Press, 1998). **Laurie Garrett,** *The Coming Plague* (New York: Penguin Books, 1994). **Joseph Gibaldi,** *MLA Handbook for Writers of Research Papers* (5th ed., New York: Modern Language Association of America, 1999), p. xiii. **Frank Goddio,** "San Diego: An Account of Adventure, Deceit, and Intrigue," *National Geographic,* 1994.

(Credits continue on p. 225-R)

SECTION 1
Writing and Reading

Voices from the Community

" Every story is an act of trust between a writer and a reader; each story, in the end, is social. Whatever a writer sets down can harm or help the community of which he or she is a part. **"**

Barry Lopez, "A Voice," *About This Life: Journeys on the Threshold of Memory*

1 | Writing and Reading in Communities

Whether you are drafting a history paper, a memo at work, or a neighborhood flyer, try to envision the **community of readers and writers** you are addressing—people with shared, though not necessarily identical, interests, goals, and preferences. Their expectations govern their responses to writing and can help you decide how best to shape ideas, information, and experiences you want to share with them.

Participating in academic, work, and public communities means talking, reading, and especially writing. As you communicate in these broad communities, you'll find that they share some preferences—such as favoring clear, specific writing—and differ on others, such as addressing the reader as *you*. Understanding such preferences can help you recognize readers' expectations and writers' limitations and choices.

1a Understanding your writing situation

Begin by "reading" your situation, often a specific task, occasion, project, or assignment.

- What is your purpose? What do you want or need to achieve?
- How will you relate to readers? What do they expect?
- What is your subject? What do you know, or need to know, about it?

STRATEGY Pinpoint your task.

Look over your job description or assignment. Draw a straight line under words (usually nouns) that specify a **topic.** Put a wavy line under action words (verbs) that tell what your writing needs to *do*, its **purpose.**

THREE COMMUNITIES OF READERS AND WRITERS			
	ACADEMIC	**WORK**	**PUBLIC**
GOALS	Create or exchange knowledge	Solve problems, inform, promote	Persuade, participate, inform
FORMS	Analysis, interpretation, lab report, proposal, article, bibliography	Memo, letter, ad, report, minutes, proposal, instructions	Letter, flyer, newsletter, position paper, fact sheet
WRITING CHARACTERISTICS	Reasoning, analysis, insights, evidence, detail, fair exploration	Clarity, accuracy, conciseness, focus on problem	Advocacy, evidence, shared values, recognition of others

Assignment: Analyze a magazine ad for hidden cultural assumptions. Describe what happens in the ad, noting camera angle, color, and focus.

Whatever your task and whatever your broad community (academic, work, or public), you need to address your specific readers, actual or potential. Always ask "Exactly what do my readers expect?"

STRATEGY **Analyze your readers.**

Size and familiarity. How large is your audience? How well do you know them? Are they close or distant?

Community. Which expectations of readers are typical of the community in which you are writing?

Knowledge. What are your readers likely to know about your topic? What do they want or need to know?

Social context. What defines your readers socially, culturally, or educationally? How do they think?

Power. Are your readers peers or superiors? What do they expect you to do? What do you expect them to do?

1b Focusing on writing processes

Experienced writers expect to use all the composing stages.

Discovering and planning. Begin by looking for a promising topic.

STRATEGY Generate ideas.

- **Freewrite** by writing quickly by hand or at the computer for five or ten minutes. Don't stop; just slip into engaging ideas.
- Try **focused freewriting,** exploring a specific idea.
- Ask **strategic questions** to stir memories and suggest what to gather. Begin with *what, why,* and *why not.* Next try *who, where, when, how.*
- Use **interactive prompts** from the Web, computer lab, tutoring center, or your software.

Move toward a design or structure to guide your drafting.

STRATEGY Focus and organize.

- Try **clustering.** Write an idea at the center of a page, and jot down random associations. Circle key ideas; add lines to connect them.
- **List ideas and details** you want to discuss.
- **Chunk** related points and material in computer files (organized by topic or by section of the paper).
- Consider a **formal outline** (numbered and lettered sections) or a **working outline** (introduction, body, conclusion) to order points.

Drafting. Begin drafting once you have a main idea (or **thesis,** see 2a) and a general structure. Draft quickly; don't worry about perfect sentences. Or try **semidrafting,** writing until you stall out, noting *etc.* or a list instead of full text, and moving on to the next point.

Revising, editing, proofreading. Revision means critically *reading* and *reworking.* It precedes fine-tuning sentences (**editing**) or **proofreading** to check for small errors.

REVISING, EDITING, AND PROOFREADING

Major revision. Redraft passages, reorganize, add, and delete.

Minor revision. Adopt a reader's point of view. Rework illogical, wordy, or weak passages.

Collaborative revision. Ask peers to suggest improvements.

Editing. Improve clarity, style, and economy; check grammar, sentence structure, wording, punctuation, and mechanics.

Proofreading. Focus on details and final appearance, especially spelling, punctuation, and typing errors.

1c Reading analytically and critically

Good writing often builds on what others have written.

Reading analytically. Concentrate on understanding the content of the article, book, or Web page. (See p. 260-T.)

STRATEGY Discover what a text says.

- How can you sum up or restate its ideas in your own words?
- What are its major ideas, insights, and persuasive points?
- How does the reading relate to others on the topic?

Reading critically. Analyze as you add your own insights.

STRATEGY Interact with a text.

Question. What do you want or need to know?

Synthesize. How does it relate to other views? What other views does it acknowledge (or fail to anticipate)?

Interpret. What does the writer mean or imply? What do you conclude about the text's outlook or bias?

Assess. How do you evaluate its value and accuracy? How does it compare to other texts that are read in the community?

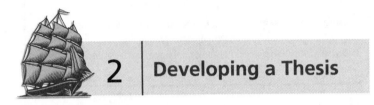

2 | Developing a Thesis

Most writing needs a clear **thesis**—a main idea, insight, or opinion that you wish to share. Announcing it in a **thesis statement** helps readers follow your reasoning and helps you organize and maintain focus.

2a Creating a thesis statement

You may choose to state your thesis near the beginning to guide readers, perhaps after introducing your topic and giving any needed background. Begin with a **rough thesis,** a sentence (or two) that identifies your perspective and states your assertion, conclusion, or opinion.

VAGUE TOPIC	Ritalin
STILL A TOPIC	The use of Ritalin for kids
STILL A TOPIC (NO ASSERTION)	Problems of Ritalin for kids with attention-deficit disorder (ADD)
	READER'S REACTION: But what should parents do?
ROUGH THESIS (ASSERTION)	Parents should be careful about Ritalin for kids with ADD.

Extend a rough thesis, making it more precise and complex. For example, what stance should parents take: Avoid Ritalin? Use it cautiously?

EXTENDED THESIS   Although Ritalin is widely used to treat children with ADD, parents should not rely too heavily on such drugs until they have explored both their child's problem and all treatment options.

STRATEGY **Sharpen your thesis until your final draft.**

Treat your thesis as tentative. Refine it to offer a clear assertion—focused, limited, and yet complex enough to warrant readers' attention.

2b Designing an appropriate thesis

Refine your thesis to suit your purpose or readers.

General thesis. Readers will expect to discover your conclusions or special perspectives.

Sooner or later, teenagers stop listening to parents and turn to each other for advice, sometimes with disastrous results.

Informative thesis. Readers will expect to learn why this information is of interest and how you'll organize it.

For parents choosing kids' videos based on their moral lessons, the job of selection is simplified by watching for three main categories of videos.

Argumentative thesis. Readers will expect your opinion, perhaps with other views on the issue, too.

Although bioengineered crops may pose some dangers, their potential for combating worldwide hunger justifies their careful use.

Academic thesis. Readers will expect you to state your specific conclusion and a plan to support it in terms that fit the field.

My survey of wedding announcements in local newspapers from 1960 to 2000 indicates that religious background and ethnicity have decreased in importance as factors in mate selection.

3 | Providing Support and Reasoning Clearly

Whether exploring an academic topic, making a recommendation at work, or urging people to take a stand on an issue, the path your thinking takes is called a **chain of reasoning.** Readers will find your writing logical and convincing if it's careful and critical, providing details and support suitable for your subject, purpose, and community.

3a Reasoning critically

What processes support critical reasoning?

- Exploring a question, problem, or experience
- Uniting ideas and information to reach a conclusion
- Focusing on the end point of the chain of reasoning—the main conclusion—often your thesis statement

---

TYPES OF CONCLUSIONS YOU MIGHT DRAW

Interpretations of meaning (experience, literature, film), importance (current event, history), or causes and effects (problem, event)

Analyses of elements (problem, situation, phenomenon, subject)

Propositions about an issue, problem, or policy

Judgments about "rightness" or "wrongness" (action, policy), quality (performance, creative work), or effectiveness (solution, course of action)

Recommendations for guidelines, policies, or responses

Warnings about consequences of action or inaction

CRITICAL REASONING IN THREE MAJOR COMMUNITIES			
	ACADEMIC	**WORK**	**PUBLIC**
GOAL	Analysis of text, phenomenon, or creative work to interpret, explain, or offer insights	Analysis of problems to supply information and propose solutions	Participation in democratic processes to contribute, inform, or persuade
REASONING PROCESS	Detailed reasoning, often explained with tight logic leading to conclusions	Accurate analysis of problem or need with clear explanation of solution	Plausible reasoning to support own point of view without ranting
SPECIAL INTERESTS	Citations of others as well as insights beyond common knowledge	Sharp focus on task, problem, or goal that promotes organization	Shared values and goals, often local, that support a cause or policy
EVIDENCE	Specific references to detailed evidence, presented to support conclusions	Sufficient evidence to show the problem's importance and justify a solution	Relevant evidence, often local, to substantiate views and probabilities
VIEWPOINT	Insightful but balanced, recognizing and explaining other views	Task-oriented but aware of alternatives and likely results	Partisan but fair, recognizing other interests and goals

STRATEGY Focus on your conclusions.

List all your conclusions, interpretations, or opinions. What others come to mind? Which are main and which secondary? What explanation or evidence connects these points? Does each lead logically to the next?

3b Providing support

A convincing chain of reasoning gives readers information that supports generalizations. **Information** includes facts of all kinds—examples, data, details, quotations—that you present as reliable, confirmable, or generally undisputed. **Generalizations** are conclusions based on and supported by information. Information turns into **evidence** when it's used to persuade a reader that an idea is reasonable.

TYPES OF EVIDENCE

Examples of an event, idea, person, or place, brief or extended, from personal experience or research

Details of an idea, place, situation, or phenomenon

Information about times, places, participants, numbers, consequences, surroundings, and relationships

Statistics, perhaps presented in tables or charts

Background on context, history, or effects

Quotations from experts, participants, or other writers

3c Evaluating support

Assess evidence critically. How **abundant** is it? Is it **sufficient** to support conclusions? Is it **relevant, accurate,** and **well documented**?

STRATEGY Align your evidence with your thesis.

General thesis. Supply evidence that fits your claim and readers' expectations (statistics, interviews, examples from experience).

Informative thesis. Give evidence showing a subject's elements.

Argumentative thesis. Supply information, examples, and quotations to support your stand, answer objections, and refute opposing views.

Academic thesis. Provide evidence that meets the discipline's standards; cite contributions of others.

4 | Paragraphing for Readers

Every time you indent to begin a new paragraph, you signal academic, workplace, or public readers to watch for a shift in topic or emphasis.

4a Focusing paragraphs

A **focused paragraph** has a clear topic and main idea that guide readers through the specifics of your discussion.

STRATEGY Check your paragraph focus.

- What is your main point in this paragraph?
- How many different ideas does it cover?
- Does it elaborate on the main idea? Do details fit?
- Have you announced your focus to readers? Where?

Help readers recognize a paragraph's focus by stating your topic and main idea or perspective in a **topic sentence.** Place this sentence at a paragraph's end, leave it unstated but clearly implied, or add a clarifying sentence to explain further. When you want readers to grasp the point right away, put this sentence first.

> When writing jokes, it's a good idea to avoid vague generalizations. Don't just talk about "fruit" when you can talk about "an apple." Strong writing creates a single image for everyone in the crowd, each person imagining a very similar thing. But when you say "fruit," people are either imagining several different kinds of fruit or they aren't really thinking of anything in particular, and both things can significantly reduce their emotional investment in the joke. But when you say "an apple," everyone has *a clear picture,* and thus a feeling.
>
> —Jay Sankey, "Zen and the Art of Stand-Up Comedy"

4b Making paragraphs coherent

A paragraph is **coherent** if each sentence leads clearly to the next, forming an easy-to-understand arrangement. When sentences are out of logical order or jump abruptly, readers may struggle to follow the thought.

STRATEGY Check your paragraph coherence.

- Does the paragraph repeat key words and synonyms naming the topic and main points? Do these words begin or end sentences, or are they buried in the middle?
- What transition words relate sentences?
- What parallel structures emphasize similar ideas?
- Are ideas and details arranged logically?

Place key words to keep readers aware of the arrangement of ideas.

People married for a long time often develop similar **facial features. Younger couples** display only chance resemblances between their **faces.** Because **they** share emotions for many years, however, **older couples** acquire similar **expressions.**

USEFUL TRANSITIONS FOR SHOWING RELATIONSHIPS

Time and sequence: next, later, after, meanwhile, while, immediately, earlier, first, second, third, shortly, in the future, subsequently, soon, since, finally, last, as long as, at that time

Comparison: likewise, similarly, also, again, in comparison

Contrast: in contrast, on the one hand . . . on the other hand, however, although, yet, but, nevertheless, at the same time, regardless

Examples: for example, for instance, such as, thus, namely, specifically, to illustrate

Cause and effect: as a result, consequently, due to, for this reason, accordingly, if . . . then, as a consequence

Place: next to, above, behind, beyond, between, here, there, opposite, to the right, in the background, over, under

Addition: and, too, moreover, in addition, besides, next, also, finally

Concession: of course, naturally, granted, it is true that, certainly

Conclusion: in conclusion, as a result, as the data show

Repetition: in other words, once again, to repeat

Summary: on the whole, to sum up, in short, therefore

4c Developing paragraphs

Paragraph development provides the informative examples, facts, details, explanations, or arguments readers expect to support a conclusion.

UNDERDEVELOPED

Recycling is always a good idea—or *almost* always. Recycling some products, even paper, may require more energy from fossil fuels and more valuable natural resources than making them the first time.

READER'S REACTION: I need to know more before I agree. Which products? How much energy does recycling take? What resources are consumed?

STRATEGY **Check your paragraph development.**

Highlight the material that develops your paragraph. Do you present enough to *inform* readers? Do you adequately *support* generalizations?

Patterns for development help you accomplish tasks in ways that readers will easily recognize.

PATTERNS FOR PARAGRAPH DEVELOPMENT

Narrating: tell a story or anecdote; recreate events

Describing: provide detail about a scene, object, character, or feeling

Comparing and contrasting: explore similarities or differences; evaluate alternatives

Explaining a process: provide directions; explain how a mechanism, procedure, or natural process operates

Dividing: separate into parts; explore their relationships

Classifying: sort into groups; explain their relationships

Defining: explain a term; illustrate a concept

Analyzing causes and effects: consider why something did or might happen

5 | Matching Style to Community

Should you use *I* or *we*—or *you*? Should you add technical terms? Such choices depend less on your "voice" than on **community style**— preferences taken for granted by communities of readers and writers.

5a Recognizing community style

Community style can help you decide what readers expect and what options you have as a writer.

Values. Do writers treat or ignore values and emotions? Do writers and readers share values or differ?

Language. What **diction**—word choices—do readers favor: vivid or neutral phrases, logical or informal links, technical or everyday terms?

Formality. Do readers expect writing that is formal, complicated, and technical or relaxed and direct?

Writer's stance. How do writers identify themselves, readers, and the topic: *I, we, you, he, she, it, they*?

STYLE IN THREE MAJOR COMMUNITIES			
	ACADEMIC	**WORK**	**PUBLIC**
APPROACH	Complex, formal, or detailed analysis	Clear, everyday, or informal explanation	Emotional, value-laden, but reasoned argument
VALUES	From the discipline's knowledge base or methods	From organizational goals such as service and efficiency	From cause, issue, or group's area of interest
LANGUAGE	Technical terms and methods of the field	Plain or technical terms but little vivid, figurative wording	Lively and emotional; few technical terms and little slang
FORMALITY	Formality supports analytical approach and values of the field	Informality reflects or builds teamwork or closeness	Informality reveals personal involvement with serious issues
STANCE	Observer (*he, she, it*) or participant (*I, we*)	Team member (*we*) with personal concern (*I, you*)	Involved person (*I, you*) or representative (*we, you*)
DISTANCE	Objective and dispassionate, not personal or emotional	Supportive, committed closeness with mutual respect	Passionate and personal about cause, issue, or group

Distance. Is a writer typically distant or involved, insider or outsider, participant or observer?

5b Adjusting to community style

Examine your community's style as you read typical documents. For example, academic writers tend to rely on formal analysis using a discipline's terms and methods. Often distant observers, they may use *I*, depending on the field, but seldom address readers directly. In contrast, work communities share values such as efficiency and service, often using *we* to build teamwork. In public exchanges, writers may be dedicated partisans, speaking individually (*I*) or collectively (*we*).

6a
design

STRATEGY **Adopt the style of your community.**

- Rely on resources that respect community knowledge, approaches, and methods.
- Use terms accepted by the community.
- Look for models—other texts that illustrate acceptable formality, stance, and distance.
- Balance appeals to logic, emotion, and authorial credibility as your community expects.

6 | Designing Documents for Readers

What makes your research report, essay, or letter memorable—clear, persuasive, and easy to read? The answer often lies in document design, considering the look of the page or screen and the processes of readers.

6a Planning your document

To design documents well, learn to use layout, type, and visual aids.

STRATEGY **Sketch a mock-up version.**

- What kind of format or document do readers expect?
- How will you lay out the pages?
- How will you highlight your organization? Will you provide a table of contents? Will you use color?
- What font, typeface, and type size will you use?
- Will you integrate visual aids? Which ones?
- What are the copyright or legal issues when using others' materials?

6b Laying out your document

Layout is the arrangement of words, sentences, lists, tables, graphs, and pictures on a page or screen. Supply visual cues for readers, but don't overwhelm your text.

> **STRATEGY** Highlight to direct the reader's eye.

- Use **boldface**, *italics*, shading, rules, and boxes to signal distinctions, to connect, and to divide.
- Set off items in lists with numbers, letters, or bullets.
- Use CAPITALS, exclamation marks (!!), and other cues sparingly for emphasis. Limit underlining (especially in Web pages with links).
- Use color to meet goals (such as warning), prioritize, trace a theme or sequence, or code symbols.
- Leave **white space**—open space not filled by other design elements—to break dense text into chunks.

Headings are phrases that forecast content. Often larger and darker, they catch a reader's eye, show structure, and lead to information.

> **STRATEGY** Design useful headings.

- Be consistent, visually in font and style and verbally in parallel structure (see 24a).
- Position headings uniformly (for example, center one level but begin another at the left margin).
- Add white space between headings and text.
- Orient headings to your task or readers: **Deducting Student Loan Interest,** not **Student Loans.**

6c Using type features

Consider readers' expectations as you judiciously use software options.

Type size and weight. Both 10- and 12-point type are easy to read; the latter is most common in academic papers. Save sizes above 12 points for special purposes (visuals, flyers, posters). Type weight (letter width and stroke thickness) can also be used to highlight.

8 point   10 point   12 point   16 point

Typefaces. Serif fonts have "little feet" or small strokes at the end of each letterform. Sans serif fonts lack them.

N   Serif   N   Sans serif

Readers tend to find serif type easier to read in text while sans serif works well in titles, headings, labels, and material onscreen. Reserve decorative fonts for brochures, invitations, or posters.

6d Using visuals

Visual aids or graphics—drawings, diagrams, photographs—can speed communication. **Tables** order text or numbers in columns and rows. **Graphs** rely on two labeled axes (vertical and horizontal), using lines or bars to relate variables. **Pie charts** show percentages of a whole.

> **STRATEGY** Integrate visuals with text.
> - Choose simple visual aids that make a point; avoid decorative filler.
> - Place a visual near related text; connect it verbally.
> - Label all graphics as figures (except for tables), number them, and supply short, accurate captions.
> - Credit sources for all borrowed graphics.

6e Sample documents

The following samples show document design in action.

Sample Academic Paper, MLA Format

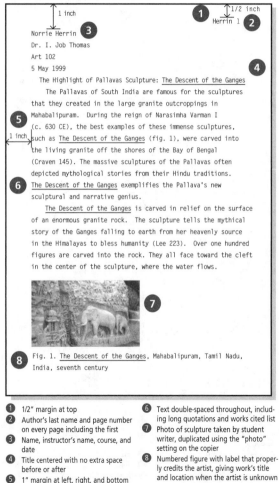

6e
design

1 inch

1/2 inch

Herrin 1

Norrie Herrin

Dr. I. Job Thomas

Art 102

5 May 1999

The Highlight of Pallavas Sculpture: The Descent of the Ganges

The Pallavas of South India are famous for the sculptures

that they created in the large granite outcroppings in

Mahabalipuram. During the reign of Narasimha Varman I

(c. 630 CE), the best examples of these immense sculptures,

1 inch such as The Descent of the Ganges (fig. 1), were carved into

the living granite off the shores of the Bay of Bengal

(Craven 145). The massive sculptures of the Pallavas often

depicted mythological stories from their Hindu traditions.

The Descent of the Ganges exemplifies the Pallava's new

sculptural and narrative genius.

The Descent of the Ganges is carved in relief on the surface

of an enormous granite rock. The sculpture tells the mythical

story of the Ganges falling to earth from her heavenly source

in the Himalayas to bless humanity (Lee 223). Over one hundred

figures are carved into the rock. They all face toward the cleft

in the center of the sculpture, where the water flows.

Fig. 1. The Descent of the Ganges, Mahabalipuram, Tamil Nadu,
India, seventh century

1 1/2" margin at top

2 Author's last name and page number on every page including the first

3 Name, instructor's name, course, and date

4 Title centered with no extra space before or after

5 1" margin at left, right, and bottom

6 Text double-spaced throughout, including long quotations and works cited list

7 Photo of sculpture taken by student writer, duplicated using the "photo" setting on the copier

8 Numbered figure with label that properly credits the artist, giving work's title and location when the artist is unknown

Sample Workplace Letter of Application

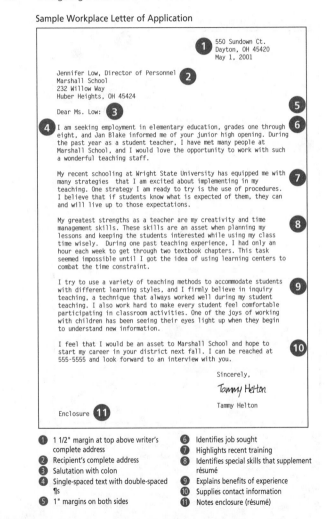

550 Sundown Ct.
Dayton, OH 45420
May 1, 2001

Jennifer Low, Director of Personnel
Marshall School
232 Willow Way
Huber Heights, OH 45424

Dear Ms. Low:

I am seeking employment in elementary education, grades one through eight, and Jan Blake informed me of your junior high opening. During the past year as a student teacher, I have met many people at Marshall School, and I would love the opportunity to work with such a wonderful teaching staff.

My recent schooling at Wright State University has equipped me with many strategies that I am excited about implementing in my teaching. One strategy I am ready to try is the use of procedures. I believe that if students know what is expected of them, they can and will live up to those expectations.

My greatest strengths as a teacher are my creativity and time management skills. These skills are an asset when planning my lessons and keeping the students interested while using my class time wisely. During one past teaching experience, I had only an hour each week to get through two textbook chapters. This task seemed impossible until I got the idea of using learning centers to combat the time constraint.

I try to use a variety of teaching methods to accommodate students with different learning styles, and I firmly believe in inquiry teaching, a technique that always worked well during my student teaching. I also work hard to make every student feel comfortable participating in classroom activities. One of the joys of working with children has been seeing their eyes light up when they begin to understand new information.

I feel that I would be an asset to Marshall School and hope to start my career in your district next fall. I can be reached at 555-5555 and look forward to an interview with you.

Sincerely,

Tammy Helton

Tammy Helton

Enclosure

1. 1 1/2" margin at top above writer's complete address
2. Recipient's complete address
3. Salutation with colon
4. Single-spaced text with double-spaced ¶s
5. 1" margins on both sides
6. Identifies job sought
7. Highlights recent training
8. Identifies special skills that supplement résumé
9. Explains benefits of experience
10. Supplies contact information
11. Notes enclosure (résumé)

Sample Workplace Résumé

Tammy Jo Helton
550 Sundown Ct., Dayton, OH 45420
453-555-5555   TJ@mailnow.com

CERTIFICATION
Elementary Education (grades 1-8)
Bachelor of Arts, August 2001, Wright State University, Dayton, OH

EDUCATION
Wright State University, 1998-2001, College of Education
Sinclair Community College, 1997-1998, general education
Wayne High School, 1997 graduate, college preparatory

AWARDS
Phi Kappa Phi National Honor Society 2000, 2001
Dean's list 1999, 2000, 2001

TEACHING EXPERIENCE

Student Teaching
Seventh grade physical science, L.T. Ball Junior High, Tipp City, OH
Planned and implemented lessons while maintaining classroom control.

Observation
Shilohview, Trotwood, OH
Implemented preplanned lessons.

Teaching
Sixth grade religious education class, Dayton, OH
Currently responsible for planning and implementing lessons.

WORK EXPERIENCE
Goal Line Sports Grill, 1998-present: Server, cash register, supervisor
Frisch's Big Boy, 1996-1998: Server, inventory, preparation
Shilohview Park, 1995-1997: Park Counselor, activity planner

INTERESTS AND ACTIVITIES
Took dance lessons for 10 years; played drums in the school band.

References available on request.

① Centers name, address, phone, and email address
② Uses bold capitals for main headings
③ Begins with required teaching credential
④ Summarizes education and awards
⑤ Organizes experience to show skills
⑥ Uses reverse chronological order
⑦ Adds optional information

Sample Public Poster

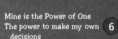

THE POWER OF ONE
Alcohol Awareness Week
March 1 – 4, 1999 • UNC Charlotte

SPECIAL EVENTS:

MONDAY, MARCH 1ST
Alcohol Insanity Tour '99
with Wendi Foxx
Nationally renowned comedienne
Wendi Foxx will entertain with Alcohol
Aware Educational Comedy.
McKnight Hall 8pm

TUESDAY, MARCH 2ND
Copacabana Mocktail Bar
Representatives from RSA and SGA
will provide refreshing alcohol-free
"mocktails" in a tropical setting right
here on campus!
After Hours 11:30am-1:30pm

WEDNESDAY, MARCH 3RD
DUI: Decisions
Under the Influence
Campus Police will demonstrate the
hazards of drinking with sobriety
exercises performed on real life
students.
Poplar Hall 2nd floor 8pm

THURSDAY, MARCH 4TH
Pledge Card Drive
Join the campus community in
pledging not to drink and drive.
Belk Tower 11am-3pm

Sponsored by the Department of Housing &
Residence Life, Resident Students

Mine is the Power of One
The power to make my own
   decisions
The power to achieve all of my
   goals

Mine is the Power of One
The power to create the life I want
The power to impact the lives of
   others

Mine is the Power of One
The power to set responsible limits
The power to drink without
   driving

The Power that is Mine
Comes from within

The Power that is Mine

---

1. Unusual font drawing attention to headline
2. Date and description of the event prominently placed
3. Open space keeping focus on key elements
4. Clear format for scheduling information
5. Interesting original artwork
6. Poem in more legible font that complements the headline

SECTION 2
Conducting Research

Voices from the Community

❝ There's plenty of room in the world of research for opinion. But opinion supported by facts has more impact and credibility. Researchers and professional writers need accurate statistics, authoritative quotations, historical background, scholarly conjecture, biographical tidbits, arcane facts, and detailed explanations of every process, theory, concept, methodology, and function imaginable. Research adds authority and color to writing. ❞

Ellen Metter, *Facts in a Flash: A Research Guide for Writers*

7 | Using Research Strategies

You may be in the library working on your psychology paper on stress, searching the Web about company-sponsored child care, or surveying neighbors on new city recreation options. Each task raises its own questions and requires different research strategies, sources, and forms for turning inquiry into writing. Each draws on its own narrow research community but addresses a broader audience—academic, work, or public.

7a Recognizing research communities

Successful research writing goes beyond simply conveying information. By blending their own insights with material from print, electronic, or field sources, researchers increase readers' understanding. Writers and readers together ideally form a **research community,** a web of people and texts preserving and adding to knowledge of a subject.

READERS AND WRITERS IN A RESEARCH COMMUNITY

- Share a perspective and focus, a **research topic**
- Agree on **research questions** worth asking and set goals for gathering and examining information
- Use shared terms, **keywords** that form a **research thread** linking topics and resources

---

7b Recognizing research topics

Your assignment may launch your inquiry. It may specify the deadlines, format, and sources expected by your teacher, supervisor, or organization.

COMMUNITY GOALS FOR RESEARCH			
	ACADEMIC	**WORK**	**PUBLIC**
GOALS	Explain, interpret, analyze, synthesize	Document problems, propose, improve	Support policy or action
READER EXPECTATIONS	Detailed evidence, varied sources	Clear, precise, direct information	Accessible, fair persuasion
TYPICAL QUESTIONS	What does it mean? How does it happen?	What is the problem? How can we solve it?	How can we improve a policy or situation?
TYPICAL FORMS	Paper to interpret or inform	Proposal, feasibility study	Speech, pamphlet, letter
SAMPLE TOPIC	Gender roles in ads	Worldwide marketing	Animal testing
SAMPLE QUESTION ON COSMETICS	What gender roles do ads reinforce?	How can we develop local packaging?	Are animal tests of cosmetics necessary?

STRATEGY Begin your inquiry with questions.

- What problem, issue, question, or event piques your curiosity?
- What new, contradictory, or intriguing ideas turn up as you read?
- What tantalizing ideas arise as you surf the Web, join a class discussion, or meet in a work or public setting?
- What would your readers also like to know?

7c Identifying keywords in your research community

As you consider research topics, note recurring words (*alcohol*), names (*John Glenn*), and phrases (*early childhood*). Libraries, search engines, and databases use such terms to categorize and access information.

STRATEGY Use keywords to maintain your focus.

- Write down all the keywords that might refer to your topic. Note synonyms (*maturation* for *growth*).

- Refine your list as you investigate. Add keywords used by print sources, search engines, or your librarian; drop those used rarely. Use this list to search library catalogs, bibliographies, databases, and the Web.
- If your keywords produce too many sources, look for more precise terms used in your community.
- Integrate your keywords into your research questions. Use them to label and group materials, organize your draft, and shape your thesis.

7d Developing research questions

7d
resrch

Research questions help you focus as you filter information and lead to your **thesis,** the main idea that you explore, support, or illustrate.

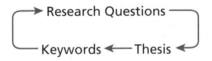

Academic. What do experts ask or say about your topic? Do you agree or disagree? What can you add? What ambiguities remain?

Work. What is the problem or situation? What do you propose? Why will it work, work better, or cost less?

Public. What policy or program do you propose? Who does it benefit? Why? What might its effects be?

Summer Arrigo-Nelson and Jennifer Figliozzi developed these research questions on student drinking for a report on a campus problem.

- Will students with permission to drink at home have different drinking behaviors at college than those without such permission?
- Do students feel that a correlation exists between drinking behaviors at home and at college?

STRATEGY **State your research questions early.**

- Aim for two or three direct questions, and embed your keywords.
- Pose questions without clear answers, not with an obvious consensus.
- Design questions that will matter to your community.

7e Selecting resources for a working bibliography

As you consult encyclopedias, indexes, catalogs, and search engines (see 8a), build a **working bibliography** of possible sources. Work with your research questions nearby; include only sources that help address them.

7f
resrch

Include

- More sources than needed, allowing for those not available or useful
- Items whose titles or lengths suggest rich and relevant resources
- Recent and varied sources, from broad surveys to focused studies
- Sources from bibliographies with *annotations* or search engines with *abstracts* that summarize content and utility

Exclude

- Sources that may be difficult to obtain or with doubtful credibility (see 9c–d)
- Sources with a questionable connection to your topic

7f Keeping track of your sources and notes

Select a system for recording bibliographic information and taking reading notes (see 9a) so you can easily document sources. Link your notes to keywords, research questions, and page numbers in sources.

Notecards. If you prefer cards—easy to group or add—write each bibliography entry on a 3" × 5" card and each reading note on a 4" × 6".

Research notebook. In a notebook you can add marginal notes, attach colored dots or flags, or duplicate pages to cut up as you organize.

Electronic notes. Software files that resemble onscreen cards easily transfer to a reference list or draft. Some programs will format entries using the style you select. Be sure to record these points.

BOOKS	ARTICLES	ELECTRONIC SOURCES
Author(s), editor(s), translator(s)	Author(s)	Name of source
	Title: Subtitle	Address/URL/access route/vendor
Title: Subtitle	Periodical name	
City: publisher, date	Volume (& issue)	Date of access
Call number	Date	Person responsible for writing or posting
	Page number(s)	Any details on original publication
	Location	

7g
resrch

7g Turning inquiry into writing

After you locate (see 8b–d) and read (see 9a–b) useful sources, you're ready to pull your research together and think strategically.

STRATEGY **Align your research with your purpose.**

- Consider what you want your readers to learn, do, or feel.
- Place your research questions in a trial sequence. Refine them.
- State, extend, and modify your rough thesis. Try breaking it into easy-to-read sentences, organizing around its parts, or restating it to help readers follow your reasoning. (See 2a–b.)
- Analyze and respond to your readers' possible reactions.
- Group your materials and arrange them in sequence—beginning, middle, and end. Connect the chunks.
- Try drafting your introduction and conclusion first, focusing on your research questions. Engage readers; keep them thinking.
- Draft the middle so readers can follow your reasoning, see your evidence, and accept your conclusions. Don't just pack in details.
- Ask readers to respond to a draft. Revise, edit, proofread (1b), and design your document (see 6a–d). Quote accurately, cite page numbers and authors correctly, and check your documentation form.

8 | Finding Print and Electronic Resources

Using a careful and thorough search strategy, you will probably uncover more sources than you can use.

8a Developing search strategies

A **search strategy** begins with your topic and research questions (see 7b–d). It helps you select, examine, and evaluate appropriate resources.

- **Library research** focuses on print or electronic books, articles, microforms, databases, recordings, and art. It calls on your skill with reference systems. (It also rewards your effort with prescreened sources selected, purchased, or gathered by library professionals.)
- **Electronic or online research** focuses on texts, data, graphics, audio, and film. It calls on your skill with software and search engines.
- **Field research** draws on artifacts, events, and oral texts. It calls on your skill with data from interviews, surveys, and observations.

Primary sources provide information in original (or close-to-original) form: historical and literary texts, messages, letters, videos, survey results, and other data with little or no interpretation by the gatherer. Analyze, interpret, and relate such sources to your research questions. **Secondary sources** explain, analyze, summarize, or interpret primary sources, telling you what others have said and what issues are debated in a given community. You generally need to interpret, compare, synthesize, or evaluate them in relation to your own questions.

STRATEGY Design your own search strategy.

- **Plan.** Identify types of research, possible sources, and stages in your process (find general sources, state research questions, and so on).

- **Focus.** Keep your keywords, research questions, and search strategies handy at the library or computer.
- **Direct your work.** Find any required kind or number of sources. Balance library resources (usually evaluated before publication) with Web sites (may be unreliable). Move from preliminary sources that suggest questions to general sources that supply background to specialized sources that support your interpretations.
- **Reflect and redirect.** Revise your research questions, search strategy, and keywords as your research evolves.

8b
source

8b Finding print and electronic references

Almost all fields of academic, work, or public interest are represented by reliable print or online references. Visit your library—or its home page—to explore its resources. Start with **ready references,** general encyclopedias, atlases, dictionaries, and statistical abstracts. Then turn to **specialized encyclopedias and dictionaries,** as varied as *Current Biography; Encyclopedia of Pop, Rock, and Soul;* and the *McGraw-Hill Encyclopedia of Science and Technology.* Check useful **bibliographies,** source compilations such as the *MLA International Bibliography* on language and literature or *International Bibliography of the Social Sciences.*

STRATEGY Talk to information specialists.

As the people in an organization with the most training in managing information, reference librarians can help you refine a search strategy, improve keyword searches, and locate materials on campus or on loan.

Periodicals appear at set periods of time with articles by many authors. **Online periodicals** on the Internet may place past issues or articles in electronic archives; other **Web sites** act like periodicals, offering selected articles, but they may add material as available or as the site is updated.

	MAGAZINES	**JOURNALS**	**NEWSPAPERS**
READERS	General public, special interest	Academics, professionals	Local, national, special interest
WRITERS	Staff, nonexperts	Experts	Journalists
FREQUENCY	Month, week	Quarter, month	Day, week, month
PAGINATION	Issue	Volume, issue	Section
FOCUS	Useful, short articles	Research findings	Timely or current news
REVIEWERS	Editors	Peer readers	Section editor
ADS	General, topical	Professional	General, local
FORMAT	Color, sidebars, photos, cover	Little color, text, data	Some color, columns, headlines

8c
source

Through your library, Internet service, or search engines, you can access **periodical indexes,** some of which supply brief summaries (or abstracts). Using indexes from varied fields can bring your research the benefits of **triangulation,** using multiple sources to enhance accuracy.

Your library will offer access to **general indexes** such as *Academic Index, InfoTrac, OCLC/World Catalog, PAIS (Public Affairs, Information Services),* or *NewsBank.* Academic libraries also supply **specialized indexes** such as *BIZZ (Business Index), Government Documents Catalog Service (GDCS/ GPO Index), Current Index to Journals in Education (CIJE), Social Sciences Index,* or *Biological and Agricultural Index.*

Indexes of electronic databases further expand your access to resources. To find those on your topic, consult your librarian or a guide such as the *Gale Directory of Databases* or the *Federal Database Finder.*

8c Tapping library resources

First identify resources, then find them. Start with the library home page or **online catalog.** Search for an *author's name,* the *title* of a work or periodical, or a *keyword.* If you find several items (each listed in a **brief**

display), click on one to call up its **full display**. You may also expand a search to related topics, authors, or works or follow related links (see 8e). Print or record your results, including call numbers and locations.

SEARCH TYPE		SEQUENCE OF SEARCH RESULTS		
Name, title, subject	→	Brief display	→	Full display
Related topics	→	Brief display	→	Full display
Browser, links	→	Indexes, resources	→	Entry displays

Government documents include general and technical reports, pamphlets, and regulations issued by Congress, federal agencies, and state or local governments. The *Monthly Catalog of U.S. Government Publications* can help direct your search, as can the *Government Information Sharing Project* <http://govinfo.kerr.orst.edu>, *Library of Congress* <http://www.loc.gov>, and *Thomas Legislative Information* site <http://thomas.loc.gov>.

Special collections house many documents, including those on local history. **Audiovisual collections** contain tapes, films, and recordings. **Microform collections** contain copies of periodicals and documents.

8d
source

8d Finding Web and Internet resources

The **Internet** links researchers through email, discussion groups, and Web sites. Online materials range from well-researched academic essays to hasty messages. (See 8f and 9d on evaluating online resources.)

You can access Web documents (**pages**) or collections of pages (**sites**) using a **browser,** such as *Netscape Navigator* or *Internet Explorer.* Enter the Web page's address, known as a **URL** (Uniform Resource Locator), or follow links embedded in an online text.

Search engines. Some Web sites collect and categorize links, providing keyword search tools for finding sources. Access popular **search engines** through your browser or their URLs.

All The Web	http://www.alltheweb.com
AltaVista	http://www.altavista.com
DogPile	http://www.dogpile.com

Google	http://www.google.com
HotBot	http://hotbot.lycos.com
MetaCrawler	http://www.go2net.com

When you use a search engine, you search its database, which catalogs items from the Net. Use several search engines because each database contains different information. You'll need to evaluate whatever you find, but you may locate prescreened material related to your research questions at smaller, more scholarly sites such as these.

BUBL Information Service	http://bubl.ac.uk
Infomine	http://infomine.ucr.edu/
Librarian's Index	http://lii.org
* to the Internet*	
The WWW Virtual Library	http://www.vlib.org

8e
source

Electronic messages and postings. Electronic mail, or **email,** allows you to contact groups or individuals who can answer questions or provide information. Search engines have directory services that can locate email addresses of individuals, and many Web pages let you email the author or sponsor.

Newsgroups and **Web discussion forums** are public sites where anyone can post a message and read what others have posted. In contrast, you contact **electronic mailing lists** yourself to subscribe, and then check your email for messages. Because all these sources are conversational, they may or may not supply reliable information (see 9d).

8e Searching efficiently

Keyword searches are crucial to your research success.

STRATEGY Use keywords to focus.

- Use your research questions and keywords to select search terms. Submit these to the search engine, catalog, or index you want to use.

- Search engines find the exact words you specify. Type—and spell—carefully. Try various word forms and related terms.
- If the database contains items with keywords matching your search terms, the items will appear as your search results.
- Repeat your search, looking for useful keywords and combinations. Use your most effective clusters to search other databases.

When you search, your string of keywords or specific terms is called a **query.** Use your query to narrow a search by grouping terms, specifying those you want to combine, rule out, or treat as alternatives.

8f
source

STRATEGY Learn advanced search strategies.

If your results seem uneven—too many or too few items—click on the advanced search strategies for the search engine, catalog, or index. Many use principles of Boolean logic.

OR (expands): Search for either term
    X OR Y → documents referring to either X or Y
AND (restricts): Search for both terms
    X AND Y → documents referring to both X and Y
NOT (excludes): Search for X unless X includes Y
    X NOT Y → documents referring to X unless they refer to Y

Search engines may automatically combine terms when you enter more than one word (*college drinking policy*) or ask you to use signs (*college + alcohol*) or words (*early childhood education NOT Head Start*).

8f   Evaluating Web search results

Because anyone can place materials online, the Internet is a tremendous resource, but also a vast collection of questionable information. In general, academic readers expect you to find authoritative sites produced by people aware of the scholarly discussion. Workplace readers expect you to use sites that address an issue directly, produced by people or groups known for accuracy. Public readers expect you to rely on sites with reliable information. For all three communities, you'll need to decide whether your search results are authoritative, current, verifiable, and credible.

STRATEGY Screen your Internet search results.

- How would you categorize a resource? Is it a business or group site, a personal page, an academic article, or something else?
- Does it indicate its author or sponsor? Does the sponsor have a reputation for accuracy or expertise? What might motivate the sponsor?
- If the item is an email message or posting, does its author seem to have expertise? Is its argument logical? Is its evidence reasonable?
- If the resource is an article or essay, is it credible? Does it cite sources? Can you check their accuracy? Does it provide supporting evidence? Does it fairly present alternate perspectives or complexities?

8g
source

8g Pulling your research materials together

Finding resources is half the challenge; managing the information that you locate is the other half.

STRATEGY Organize as you track information.

- Gather your notes, copies, printouts, files, and other material.
- Sort your resources, and track down missing material.
- Use your research questions as guides to main points and subtopics. Use keywords, color codes, or stacks of material to sort by category.
- If a category contains little information, decide whether to drop it or do more research. If a category contains lots of material, decide whether to break it into subtopics.
- If you haven't found enough information, get help from a librarian, instructor, colleague, or specialist in the field.

9 | Reading and Evaluating Sources

A research project calls for two types of reading (see 1c). Read **analytically** to understand; read **critically** to interact.

9a Reading analytically: Summarize, paraphrase, synthesize

Analytical reading leads to summaries, paraphrases, quotations, and details that address research questions.

STRATEGY Compress main ideas in a short summary.

Read. Carefully underline, highlight, or note the key ideas, supporting evidence, and other information.

Scan. Reread to decide which ideas are *most* important. Figure out the text's main purpose and major sections.

Write. Sum up each section or stage of the argument or explanation in a *single sentence*, noting the key ideas. Then sum up the entire passage in a *single sentence* that captures its main point.

Combine. Merge the overall and section summaries.

Revise. Aim for logic, readability, and accuracy.

Document. Clearly indicate your source.

Summer Arrigo-Nelson and Jennifer Figliozzi used summary sentences to introduce a research question, noting sources in APA style (see 12c).

First, research has shown that adolescents who have open and close relationships with their parents use alcohol less often than do those with conflictual relationships (Sieving, 1996). For example, a survey of students in seventh through twelfth grades reported that approximately 35% of adolescent drinkers were under parental supervision while drinking (Department of Education, 1993).

A **paraphrase** presents the content and sense of a source in your own words with your own focus. To paraphrase visuals or graphics, "extract" information from them and "translate" it into your own words.

STRATEGY **Restate a source's ideas in a paraphrase.**

Read. Concentrate on both wording and content.

Write. Replace the original with your own sentences, using synonyms and equivalent phrases. You can retain names and the like.

Revise. Aim for clear sentence structure and wording so your version is easy to read and does not echo the source.

Document. Clearly indicate your source.

9a
read

Jennifer Figliozzi read this passage in a report on current alcohol abuse programs at various schools:

The university also now notifies parents when their sons or daughters violate the alcohol policy, or any other aspect of the student code of conduct. "We were hoping that the support of parents would help change students' behavior, and we believe it has," says Timothy F. Brooks, an assistant vice-president and the dean of students.

To integrate this information smoothly, Jennifer combined a paraphrase with a brief quotation and cited it using APA style (see 12a and c).

Officials at the University of Delaware thought that letting parents know when students violate regulations on alcohol use would alter students' drinking habits, and one administrator now says, "we believe it has" (Reisberg, 1998, p. A42).

An **analytical synthesis** contrasts or consolidates summaries of several sources, relating them to your research questions.

STRATEGY Relate ideas in a synthesis of sources.

Read. Read and summarize the sources individually.

Focus. Decide on the purpose of your synthesis. Sum up your conclusions about how the sources relate.

Arrange. Select a sequence for the sources.

Write. Draft your synthesis, combining summaries of the sources with conclusions about their relationships.

Revise. Rewrite so that readers can easily follow your synthesis.

Document. Clearly indicate your sources.

Summer and Jennifer used synthesis to open their paper, reviewing research that justified their research questions. (See 12c.)

Studies conducted with high school students have supported the hypothesis that positive family relationships are more likely to be associated with less frequent alcohol use among adolescents than are negative relationships. Adolescents model the limited substance use of their parents where there is a good or moderate parent-adolescent relationship (Andrews, Hops, & Duncan, 1997). Other factors the studies found to be associated with positive family relationships, along with substance use, were academic achievement, family structure, place of residence, self-esteem, and emotional tone (Martsh & Miller, 1997; Wechsler, Dowdall, Davenport, & Castillo, 1995).

9b Reading critically: Question, synthesize, interpret, assess

Critical reading develops your own insights but rests on your understanding of a source. Begin, for example, with a **question**—an academic query, unsolved work problem, or unresolved public issue.

STRATEGY Prepare a problem paragraph.

Challenge a source by noting problems, evidence, or perspectives not fully considered. State them concisely in a **problem paragraph.**

Lily Germaine prepared this note card on bodybuilding.

Tucker, pp. 389–91   Weight training & self-concept

Tucker uses "although" at least four times when summarizing
other studies. He's nice on the surface but sets his readers up
to find fault with other studies that lack objective
methodology. But he thinks he can be completely objective about
such a slippery thing as "self-concept." I really question this.

9b
read

Lily's problem paragraph incorporated her insights.

Does bodybuilding affect self-concept? Before we can answer this
question, we need to ask if we can accurately measure such a slippery
thing as "self-concept." Some researchers, like Tucker, believe that
self-concept can be accurately gauged using mathematical measurements and rigid definitions of terms. For several reasons, however,
this assumption is questionable.

Use a **critical synthesis** to explore connections among interpretations, opinions, and evidence from various sources. As for an analytical
synthesis (see 9a), provide a unified discussion of perspectives, but go
further—highlight differences and draw conclusions.

STRATEGY Synthesize to connect perspectives.

- Consider your purpose, perhaps reviewing prior academic research,
  assessing options at work, or examining positions on a public issue.
- Focus on material directly related to your central idea.
- Be true to the ideas and information in your sources.
- Use your own ideas to relate conclusions, opinions, and facts.
- Write a statement to sum up connections you observe.
- Acknowledge contradictions and alternatives.

Kimlee Cunningham used this analytical synthesis to expand her paper's key idea on recent Disney films. She followed MLA style, citing a one-page article and an online posting (see 11a and c).

It is probably an exaggeration to say that a character like Belle in Beauty and the Beast is a lot like a contemporary feminist, as one critic suggests (Showalter). However, we should not simply ignore an interpretation like this. Even if many people view a film like Beauty and the Beast (or Aladdin) as a simple love story (Hoffman), the films nonetheless grow out of the complicated values and roles that shape relationships today. Disney's contemporary portrayal of women characters shows a willingness to change with the times but also a reluctance to abandon traditional values and stereotypes.

9b
read

As you present your point of view on an academic issue, a proposal at work, or a public issue, you should interpret your sources, showing why readers should accept your views instead of theirs. **Interpretation** involves **generalizing**—reaching broad conclusions about what sources say—and **extending**—going beyond to your own views.

STRATEGY **Interpret a source's outlook and balance.**
- State your source's conclusions accurately, noting advocacy or bias.
- State your own viewpoint with supporting evidence, perhaps comparing it with that of the source.
- Add your interpretations and conclusions.

Assess sources carefully; not all are equally valuable. (See 8f, 9c–d.)

STRATEGY **Assess accuracy, credibility, and value.**
- Support reasonable judgments with examples.
- Explain judgments by comparing texts or data.
- Use your own ideas, but feel free to draw on sources that assess.

9c Evaluating sources critically

In contrast to Web sites or Internet documents, books from reputable publishers and articles in scholarly journals or well-known magazines generally are reviewed and produced with editorial checks and balances. Even so, every source, print or online, has its own point of view.

STRATEGY Evaluate all your sources.

- Does the publisher, publication, or sponsor have a reputation for balance or strong advocacy? Do other sources find the author fair?
- How accurate is the source itself? How does it use facts?
- How does the writer support statements? Do the claims go beyond the facts? Do they fit with what you know?
- Are the ideas generally consistent with those in other sources? If not, do they seem insightful or misleading?
- Does the source meet the expectations of your research community? Does it have the detail, evidence, and citations readers expect?
- Does the source document information, quotations, and ideas or clearly attribute them to the author?
- Is the source outdated? Does it cite experts with political or financial interests? Does it try to hide its viewpoint? If so, use it with caution.

9d
eval

9d Evaluating online sources critically

These Web pages show how to examine a Web site critically (see 9c).

"The Good, the Bad and the Ugly: or, Why It's a Good Idea to Evaluate Web Sources," <http://lib.nmsu.edu/instruction/eval.html>
"Thinking Critically about World Wide Web Resources," <http://www.library.ucla.edu/libraries/college/help/critical/index.htm>
"Evaluating Web Resources" (with links to checklists and examples), <http://www2.widener.edu/Wolfgram-Memorial-Library/webevaluation/webeval.htm>

STRATEGY Probe your Web material.

- Examine the affiliation, bias, design, credibility, evidence, support, documentation, and possible community reaction to any source.
- Is the material documentary (films, sounds, images, surveys, original texts)? Consider authenticity, selectivity, and relevance.
- Is the resource textual (essays, narratives, studies, articles)? Consider authorship, reasoning, support, complexity, fairness, and sources.
- Is the source peculiar to the Web (personal, educational, organizational site)? Consider genre, sponsor, motivation, and content.
- Is the resource conversational (email, discussion lists, newsgroups, forums)? Analyze it as primary material (see 8a). Look at the author's expertise, reasoning, support, and substantiation elsewhere.

9d
eval

To evaluate Web sources, ask the questions developed by Paula Mathieu and Ken McAllister for the CRITT (Critical Resources in Teaching with Technology) project at the University of Illinois at Chicago.

- **Who benefits? What difference does that make?** The Web pages at <http://www.whymilk.com>, for example, seem dedicated to the reader's health (Figure 9.1). But because this site promotes drinking milk every day, milk processors will also benefit from sales.
- **Who's talking? What difference does that make?** The "speaker" for the site's positive facts about milk is identified as "us" in the invitation to request more information. The site's privacy statement, however, identifies the site owner as the California Fluid Milk Processor Advisory Board. What might be this group's point of view? Will all the "facts" appear, especially any that question milk's goodness?

    The Web page at <http://liberator.enviroweb.org/fall94/milk.html> provides a contrary voice, linking milk to disease (see Figure 9.2 on p. 44). The article was published in *AnimaLife*, founded by an advocacy group, Cornell Students for the Ethical Treatment of Animals. The author seems to provide scientific support, but readers may find the reasoning strained and the tone impassioned.

9d
eval

1. Commercial site
2. Includes features designed to appeal to readers
3. Offers quizzes on milk
4. Advocates drinking milk
5. Uses graphics to convey information
6. Offers more information

Reader's Reaction: Why are you sharing all this? How do you benefit? How do I know this is accurate, complete information?

FIGURE 9.1   "Milk U" Web page

9d
eval

① Organizational site

② Uses title to introduce position

③ Adds graphics to highlight point of view

④ Includes statistics

⑤ Cites authority

Reader's Reaction: Given the number of milk drinkers, how serious is this risk? Isn't this view a bit extreme?

FIGURE 9.2 "Milk . . . Help Yourself" Web page

- **What's missing? What difference does that make?** The *Whymilk* site is a commercial venture promoting cow's milk. Naturally it ignores soy, goat, and other milk (and nonmilk) options. On the other hand, "Milk . . . Help Yourself" is published by a college animal rights group and omits data on milk's safety and health benefits. Each of these—like every other resource—has a point of view or vested interest that guides its selection and presentation of information.

10 | Integrating and Crediting Sources

By distinguishing your contributions from those of your sources, you'll get credit for your insights and hard work. You'll also avoid inadvertently taking credit for the work of others—a form of theft called **plagiarism**. Carefully citing sources adds to your credibility, substantiates your knowledge, and allows readers to draw on your research.

10a Documenting sources for your community

Each community has its own expectations about using sources. As you read, notice what is drawn from sources and how it is presented.

Academic. Academic readers generally expect you to acknowledge prior work, showing how your ideas fit into a research tradition. They look for authoritative evidence and documentation appropriate to the field. Try to integrate sources—emphasizing quotations, findings, currency, or other matters—as readers in a field expect.

Work. Readers at work expect brief treatment of what they know and extended treatment of what they don't (but need to). They may expect quotations, paraphrases, summaries, or visuals—all documented.

Public. Public readers may appreciate source material but be content with informal citations. But when you advocate a policy or offer controversial interpretations, readers expect fair play and accurate detail.

10b Using quotations

Select any quotation carefully, identify your source, retain its exact wording, and integrate it to support your points.

> **POSSIBLE CONTRIBUTIONS OF QUOTATIONS**
> - Bolster your conclusions with a recognized authority.
> - Convey ideas accurately, stylishly, concisely, or persuasively.
> - Provide a jumping-off point, change of pace, or vivid example.

You can quote entire sentences, with proper attribution.

> Celebrities can also play roles in our fantasy lives: "Many people admire, but do not mimic, the audacity of the rebellious rock star" (McVey 32).

Or you can embed a quotation of a few words or lines.

> Many teens were "riveted by Dylan's lyrical cynicism" (Low 124).

STRATEGY **Present quotations as readers expect.**

If you use a specific documentation style (see Section 3), check its advice on quotations and in-text citations. Here are general guidelines.

- Put the exact spoken or written words of your source in quotation marks. Introduce and connect the quotation smoothly, interpreting for readers. Mention the source in your text or a citation.

- Use a colon only after an introductory line that is a complete sentence. Use commas to set off tags such as "*X* said" that introduce or interrupt a quotation. Otherwise, use the context to determine the punctuation.
- Review related conventions: combining marks (31b), capitals (33b), and ellipses and brackets (38c–d).

Block quotations for prose. When you quote a passage longer than four lines typed (MLA style) or forty words or more (APA style), begin on the line after your introduction. Indent 1" or ten spaces (MLA style, see 11c) or ½" or five spaces (APA style, shown below). Double-space but omit quotation marks (unless they appear in the source).

10b
integ

> Perez (1998) anticipates shifts in staff training:
>> The great challenge for most school districts is to earmark sufficient funds for training personnel, not for purchasing or upgrading hardware and software. The technological revolution in the average classroom will depend to a large degree on innovation in professional development. (p. 64)

Begin the first line without further indentation if you quote from one paragraph. Otherwise, indent all paragraphs ¼" or three spaces (MLA) or any additional paragraph ½" or five spaces (APA).

Block quotations for poetry. When you quote four or more lines of poetry, begin on the line after your introduction. Indent ten spaces (1") from the left (MLA style, shown below). Double space, and don't use quotation marks unless the verse contains them.

> Donald Hall also varies line length and rhythm, as "The Black-Faced Sheep" illustrates.
>> My grandfather spent all day searching the valley
>> and edges of Ragged Mountain,
>> calling "Ke-<u>day</u>!" as if he brought you salt,
>> "Ke-<u>day</u>! Ke-<u>day</u>!" (lines 9–12)

10c Integrating sources into your text

Credit your sources, and weave their points or details into your own line of reasoning. To make your writing more sophisticated, quote selectively. Paraphrase, summarize, or synthesize instead (see 9a).

EMBEDDING SOURCE MATERIAL

- Select sound evidence that supports your purpose and thesis.
- Alternate striking short quotations with paraphrase and summary to avoid long, tedious quotations.
- Draw facts, details, and statistics from your sources as well as ideas and expressions. Credit these, too.
- Integrate sources so that your interpretation and chain of reasoning dominates and shapes the discussion.
- Don't just tack sources together assuming readers will figure out how to interpret or connect them.

Drawings, photos, tables, graphs, and charts can consolidate or explore data (see 6d). If you copy a printed visual or download one, you'll need to cite its source and may need permission to use it.

STRATEGY Integrate visuals for readers.

- Put the visual close to the relevant text without disrupting the discussion. Make sure that it explains or extends your point.
- Use clear, readable visuals in an appropriate size.
- Add labels (MLA: Table 1, Figure 1; APA: Fig. 1) (see 6d).
- Ask peers or colleagues whether your visuals are useful.

10d Avoiding plagiarism

As you quote, paraphrase, or summarize, you *must* cite sources.

- Enclose someone's exact words in quotation marks.
- Paraphrase and summarize in your own words.
- Cite the source of whatever you integrate.

Without quotation marks, the following paraphrase is too close to the original and would be seen as plagiarized.

ORIGINAL PASSAGE

Malnutrition was a widespread and increasingly severe problem throughout the least developed parts of the world in the 1970s, and would continue to be serious, occasionally reaching famine conditions, as the millennium approached. Among the cells of the human body most dependent upon a steady source of nutrients are those of the immune system, most of which live, even under ideal conditions, for only days at a time. (From Laurie Garrett, *The Coming Plague*, New York: Penguin, 1994, p. 199.)

PLAGIARIZED VERSION

In her book about emerging global diseases, Garrett points out that malnutrition can give microbes an advantage as they spread through the population. Malnutrition continues to be a **severe problem throughout the least developed parts of the world**. The human immune system contains cells that are **dependent upon a steady source of nutrients**. These cells may **live, even under ideal conditions, for only days at a time**.

The writer of the plagiarized version made only minor changes in some phrases and "lifted" others verbatim.

APPROPRIATE PARAPHRASE

In her book about emerging global diseases, Garrett points out that malnutrition can give microbes an advantage as they spread through the population. The human body contains immune cells that help to fight off various diseases. When the body is deprived of nutrients, these immune cells will weaken (Garrett 199).

10d
plag

For a paper on the general threat of global disease, the passage could simply be summarized.

APPROPRIATE SUMMARY

Malnutrition can so weaken people's immune systems that diseases they would otherwise fight off can gain an advantage (Garrett 199).

10e Deciding what to document

In general, document words, ideas, and information drawn from another person's work. Add credibility by showing your careful research, acknowledging someone's hard work, and giving others access to your sources. What needs documenting may vary with your readers. General readers may expect sources when you identify subatomic particles; physicists probably would assume this is common knowledge.

You *Must* Document

- Word-for-word (direct) quotations from a source
- Paraphrases or summaries of someone else's work, whether published or presented orally or electronically
- Ideas, opinions, and interpretations that others have developed, even those based on common knowledge
- Facts or data someone has gathered or identified, unless the information is considered common knowledge
- Information that is disputed or not widely accepted
- Visuals, recordings, performances, interviews, and the like

But *Do Not* Document

- Ideas, opinions, and interpretations that are your own
- Widely known information available in common reference works or generally seen as common knowledge
- Commonly used quotations ("To be, or not to be")

SECTION 3
Documenting Sources

Voices from the Community

❝ The *MLA Handbook for Writers of Research Papers* is designed to introduce you to the customs of a community of writers who greatly value scrupulous scholarship and the careful documentation, or recording, of research. ❞

Joseph Gibaldi, *MLA Handbook for Writers of Research Papers,* 5th ed.

❝ Rules for the preparation of manuscripts should contribute to clear communication. . . . They spare readers a distracting variety of forms throughout a work and permit readers to give full attention to content. ❞

Publication Manual of the American Psychological Association, 5th ed.

GUIDE TO MLA FORMATS

MLA Formats for In-Text (Parenthetical) Citations

1. Author's Name in Parentheses
2. Author's Name in Discussion
3. Specific Reference
4. General Reference
5. One Author
6. Two or Three Authors
7. More Than Three Authors
8. Corporate or Group Author
9. No Author Given
10. More Than One Work by the Same Author

11. Authors with the Same Name
12. Indirect Source
13. Two or More Sources in a Citation
14. Electronic or Other Nonprint Source
15. Multivolume Work
16. Literary Work
17. Bible
18. Selection in Anthology
19. Informative Footnote or Endnote

MLA Formats for List of Works Cited

Books and Works Treated as Books

1. One Author
2. Two or Three Authors
3. Four or More Authors
4. Corporate or Group Author
5. No Author Given
6. More Than One Work by the Same Author
7. One or More Editors
8. Author and Editor
9. Translator
10. Edition Following the First
11. Reprint
12. Multivolume Work
13. Work in a Series
14. Book Pre-1900
15. Book with Publisher's Imprint
16. Anthology or Collection of Articles
17. Conference Proceedings
18. Title Within a Title
19. Pamphlet
20. Dissertation (Published)

21. Dissertation (Unpublished)
22. Government Document

Articles and Selections from Periodicals and Books

23. Article in Journal Paginated by Volume
24. Article in Journal Paginated by Issue
25. Article in Weekly Magazine
26. Article in Monthly Magazine
27. Article with No Author Given
28. Article in Newspaper
29. Editorial
30. Letter to the Editor
31. Interview (Published)
32. Review
33. Article in Encyclopedia or Reference Work
34. Chapter in Edited Book or Selection in Anthology
35. More Than One Selection from Anthology or Collection

11
MLA

11 | MLA Style

The MLA (Modern Language Association) documentation style is a clear system for acknowledging your sources and directing readers to them. It has two elements: a citation in the text (usually in parentheses) and a list of works cited (at the end of the text).

These elements are simple and direct in MLA style, which emphasizes scrupulous respect for ideas, information, and quotations from sources. Use it in academic settings when you write in a humanities field or your instructor asks for simple, parenthetical documentation. Consider it in public and work settings when your audience would appreciate a clear, direct style that seldom uses footnotes or endnotes.

For more detailed discussion, see the *MLA Handbook for Writers of Research Papers* (5th ed., New York: MLA, 1999), the *MLA Style Manual and Guide to Scholarly Publishing* (2nd ed., New York: MLA, 1998), or updates posted on the MLA Web site <http://www.mla.org/>.

11a MLA in-text (parenthetical) citations

In MLA style, you include in the text information that helps readers identify and locate your source, described in full in the list of works cited at the end of the paper. Generally, an author's name is enough to identify the source. Provide this basic information in one of two places: in parentheses or in your discussion.

1. Author's Name in Parentheses

WITHIN
PARENTHESES

When people marry now, "there is an important
sense in which they don't know what they are doing"
(Giddens 46).

2. Author's Name in Discussion

PART OF
DISCUSSION

Giddens claims that when people marry now "there
is an important sense in which they don't know what
they are doing" (46).

3. Specific Reference

A **specific reference** documents words, ideas, or facts from a particular place in a source, such as the page from which you draw a quotation or paraphrase.

QUOTATION	Dolphins perceive clicking sounds "made up of 700 units of sound per second" (Bright 52).
PARAPHRASE	Bright reports that dolphins recognize patterns consisting of seven hundred clicks each second (52).

4. General Reference

A **general reference** refers to ideas or information throughout the source as a whole; it needs no page number.

WITHIN PARENTHESES	Many species of animals have complex systems of communication (Bright).
PART OF DISCUSSION	As Michael Bright observes, many species of animals have complex systems of communication.

5. One Author

According to Maureen Honey, government posters during World War II often portrayed homemakers "as vital defenders of the nation's homes" (135).

6. Two or Three Authors

The item is noted in a partial list of Francis Bacon's debts from 1603 on (Jardine and Stewart 275).

Follow the same pattern for three authors: (Norman, Fraser, and Jenko 209).

7. More Than Three Authors

Within parentheses, use *et al.* ("and others") after the name of the first author. Within your discussion, use phrases like "Chen and his colleagues observe . . . ." If you give all the names in the works cited list rather than using *et al.*, do the same in the text (see Entry 3, p. 60).

**11a
MLA**

```
More funding would encourage creative research on

complementary medicine (Chen et al. 1982).
```

8. Corporate or Group Author

If an organization is named as the author, use its name in the citation; shorten cumbersome names such as Committee of Concerned Journalists.

```
The consortium gathers American journalists at "a critical

moment" (Committee 187).
```

9. No Author Given

```
In 1993, Czechoslovakia split into the Czech Republic and

the Slovak Republic (Baedeker's 67).
```

The full title is *Baedeker's Czech/Slovak Republics.*

10. More Than One Work by the Same Author

When the list of works cited contains more than one entry by an author, add a shortened title to your citation.

```
One writer claims that "quaintness glorifies the unassuming

industriousness" in these social classes (Harris, Cute 46).
```

11. Authors with the Same Name

Add the first initial or name to distinguish the author.

```
Despite improved health information systems (J. Adams 308),

a recent report indicates that medical errors continue to

increase (D. Adams 1).
```

12. Indirect Source

Use *qtd. in* ("quoted in") for a quote or paraphrase taken from yet another source. Here, Feuch is the source of the quotation from Vitz.

For Vitz, "art, especially great art, must engage all or
almost all of the major capacities of the nervous system"
(qtd. in Feuch 65).

13. Two or More Sources in a Citation

Separate sources within a citation with a semicolon.

The different ways men and women use language can often be
traced to who has power (Tanner 83-86; Tavris 297-301).

14. Electronic or Other Nonprint Source

Identify author, title, or other information needed to find the entry in
your list of works cited. Include numbers for the page, paragraph (*par.,
pars.*), section (*sec.*), or screen (*screen*) if given. Otherwise, no number is
needed.

Offspringmag.com summarizes current research on adolescent
behavior (Boynton 2).

The heroine's mother in the film Clueless died as the result
of an accident during liposuction.

15. Multivolume Work

To cite a whole volume, add a comma after the author's name and *vol.*
before the number (Cao, vol. 4). To specify one of several volumes that
you cite, add the volume number to the text citation (Cao 4: 177).

In 1888, Lewis Carroll gave two students permission to call
their school paper Jabberwock, a made-up word from Alice's
Adventures in Wonderland (Cohen 2: 695).

16. Literary Work

After the page number in your edition add the chapter (*ch.*), part (*pt.*), or section (*sec.*) number to help readers find the passage in any edition of the work.

```
In Huckleberry Finn, Mark Twain ridicules an actor who

"would squeeze his hand on his forehead and stagger back and

kind of moan" (178; ch. 21).
```

For poems, give line numbers (lines 55–57) or both part and line numbers (4.220–23). For plays, give the act, scene, and line numbers: (Ham. 1.2.76).

17. Bible

Place a period between the chapter and verse (Mark 2.3–4). In parenthetical citations, abbreviate names with five or more letters, such as Deuteronomy: (Deut. 16.21–22).

18. Selection in Anthology

11a
MLA

For an essay, story, poem, or other selection in an anthology, cite the work's author (not the anthology's editor), but give page numbers in the anthology.

```
According to Corry, the battle for Internet censorship has

crossed party lines (112).
```

19. Informative Footnote or Endnote

When you wish to comment on a source or supply lengthy information useful to only a few readers, use a footnote or endnote. Place a superscript number (raised slightly above the line of text) at a suitable point in your paper. Then provide the note itself, with a corresponding number, as a footnote at the end of the page or as an endnote at the paper's end, before the list of works cited, on a page titled "Notes."

¹ Before changing your eating habits or beginning an

exercise program, check with your doctor.

11b MLA list of works cited

Provide readers with detailed publication information about the sources you cite in your text.

- Begin a list titled "Works Cited" on a new page right after your paper ends. If you include all the works you consulted, not just those you cited, call it "Works Consulted." (See p. 78 for a sample list.)
- Alphabetize by authors' last names; then alphabetize by title multiple works by the same author. For sources without authors, use the first main word in the title.
- Do not indent the first line of each entry; indent additional lines one-half inch or five spaces.
- Double-space the entire list. Leave a single space after a period within an entry.

Books and Works Treated as Books

Provide the author's name (last name first); underlined title; city of publication, publisher in short form (*U of Chicago P* for University of Chicago Press or *McGraw* for *McGraw-Hill, Inc.*), and year of publication.

11b
MLA

1. One Author

Twitchell, James B. <u>ADCULTusa: The Triumph of Advertising in</u>

<u>American Culture</u>. New York: Columbia UP, 1996.

2. Two or Three Authors

Kress, Gunther, and Theo van Leeuwen. <u>Reading Images: The</u>

<u>Grammar of Graphic Design</u>. London: Routledge, 1996.

3. Four or More Authors

After the first name, add *et al.* (meaning "and others").

> Bellah, Robert N., et al. <u>Habits of the Heart: Individualism</u>
>
>   <u>and Commitment in American Life</u>. Berkeley: U of California
>
>   P, 1985.

You also may give all the names; if so, list them in any parenthetical citations (see Entry 7 on p. 55).

4. Corporate or Group Author

If the organization is also the publisher, repeat its name, abbreviated if appropriate.

> Nemours Children's Clinic. <u>Diabetes and Me</u>. Wilmington, DE:
>
>   Nemours, 2001.

5. No Author Given

> <u>Guide for Authors</u>. Oxford: Blackwell, 1985.

6. More Than One Work by the Same Author

> Tannen, Deborah. <u>The Argument Culture: Moving from Debate to</u>
>
>   <u>Dialogue</u>. New York: Random, 1998.
>
> ---. <u>You Just Don't Understand: Women and Men in Conversation</u>.
>
>   New York: Ballantine, 1991.

7. One or More Editors

> Achebe, Chinua, and C. L. Innes, eds. <u>African Short Stories</u>.
>
>   London: Heinemann, 1985.

8. Author and Editor

Wardlow, Gayle Dean. <u>Chasin' That Devil Music: Searching for
the Blues</u>. Ed. Edward Komara. San Francisco: Miller
Freeman, 1998.

9. Translator

Baudrillard, Jean. <u>Cool Memories II: 1978-1990</u>. Trans. Chris
Turner. Durham: Duke UP, 1996.

10. Edition Following the First

Coe, Michael D. <u>The Maya</u>. 6th ed. New York: Thames, 1999.

11. Reprint

Ondaatje, Michael. <u>The Collected Works of Billy the Kid</u>. 1970.
Harmondsworth, Eng.: Penguin, 1984.

12. Multivolume Work

You may cite the whole work or a specific volume, ending with the total
if you wish.

Tsao, Hsueh-chin. <u>The Story of the Stone</u>. Trans. David Hawkes.
5 vols. Harmondsworth, Eng.: Penguin, 1983-86.

Tsao, Hsueh-chin. <u>The Story of the Stone</u>. Trans. David Hawkes.
Vol. 1. Harmondsworth, Eng.: Penguin, 1973. 5 vols.

13. Work in a Series

Hess, Gary R. <u>Vietnam and the United States: Origins and Legacy
of War</u>. Intl. Hist. Ser. 7. Boston: Twayne, 1990.

**11b
MLA**

14. Book Pre-1900

Darwin, Charles. <u>Descent of Man and Selection in Relation to</u>
<u>Sex</u>. New York, 1896.

15. Book with Publisher's Imprint

Sikes, Gini. <u>8 Ball Chicks: A Year in the Violent World of Girl</u>
<u>Gangs</u>. New York: Anchor-Doubleday, 1997.

Anchor is the imprint.

16. Anthology or Collection of Articles

Zipes, Jack, ed. <u>Don't Bet on the Prince: Contemporary Feminist</u>
<u>Fairy Tales in North America and England</u>. New York:
Methuen, 1986.

To cite a specific selection, see Entry 34 on page 66.

17. Conference Proceedings

<u>Childhood Obesity: Causes and Prevention</u>. Symposium Proc.,
27 Oct. 1998. Washington: Center for Nutrition Policy and
Promotion, 1999.

18. Title Within a Title

MacPherson, Pat. <u>Reflecting on</u> Jayne Eyre. London: Routledge,
1989.

Golden, Catherine, ed. <u>The Captive Imagination: A Casebook on</u>
<u>"The Yellow Wall-paper."</u> New York: Feminist, 1992.

19. Pamphlet

Vareika, William. <u>John La Farge: An American Master</u>

<u>(1835-1910)</u>. Newport: Gallery of American Art, 1989.

20. Dissertation (Published)

Said, Edward W. <u>Joseph Conrad and the Fiction of Autobiography</u>.

Diss. Harvard U, 1964. Cambridge: Harvard UP, 1966.

21. Dissertation (Unpublished)

Anku, William Oscar. "Procedures in African Drumming: A Study

of Akan/Ewe Traditions and African Drumming in

Pittsburgh." Diss. U of Pittsburgh, 1988.

22. Government Document

Sheppard, David I., and Shay Bilchick, comps. <u>Promising</u>

<u>Strategies to Reduce Gun Violence Report</u>. US Dept. of

Justice. Office of Juvenile Justice and Delinquency

Prevention. Washington: GPO, 1999.

United States. Cong. House. <u>Anti-Spamming Act of 2001</u>. 107th

Cong., 1st sess. Washington: GPO, 2001.

11b
MLA

Articles and Selections from Periodicals and Books

Provide the author's name (last name first), article title (in quotation marks), book or periodical title (underlined), and publication information (volume number for a periodical, date, page numbers). When the pages are not consecutive, give the first one with a + (48+).

23. Article in Journal Paginated by Volume

Each volume consists of several issues with continuous pagination through them all. Supply the volume number.

```
Rockwood, Bruce L. "Law, Literature, and Science Fiction: New

     Possibilities." Legal Studies Forum 23 (1999): 267-80.
```

24. Article in Journal Paginated by Issue

Each issue begins with page 1; add the issue number after the volume number.

```
Adams, Jessica. "Local Color: The Southern Plantation in

     Popular Culture." Cultural Critique 42.1 (1999): 171-87.
```

25. Article in Weekly Magazine

```
Wright, Robert. "The Power of Their Peers." Time 24 Aug.

     1998: 67.
```

26. Article in Monthly Magazine

```
Jacobson, Doranne. "Doing Lunch." Natural History Mar. 2000:

     66-69.
```

27. Article with No Author Given

```
"Horseplay." New Yorker 5 Apr. 1993: 36-38.
```

28. Article in Newspaper

For a local newspaper, add the city's name in brackets after the title unless the city is named in the title.

```
Willis, Ellen. "Steal This Myth: Why We Still Try to Re-create

     the Rush of the 60's." New York Times 20 Aug. 2000: AR1+.
```

29. Editorial

"A False Choice." Editorial. <u>Charlotte Observer</u> 16 Aug.

1998: 2C.

30. Letter to the Editor

Varley, Colin. Letter. <u>Archaeology</u> May-June 1993: 10.

31. Interview (Published)

Stewart, Martha. "'I Do Have a Brain.'" Interview with Kevin

Kelly. <u>Wired</u> Aug. 1998: 114.

32. Review

Include the reviewer and the review's title, if available.

Muñoz, José Esteban. "Citizens and Superheroes." Rev. of <u>The</u>

<u>Queen of America Goes to Washington City</u>, by Lauren

Berlant. <u>American Quarterly</u> 52 (2000): 397-404.

Hadjor, Kofi Buenor. Rev. of <u>The Silent War: Imperialism and</u>

<u>the Changing Perception of Race</u>, by Frank Furendi. <u>Journal</u>

<u>of Black Studies</u> 30 (1999): 133-35.

33. Article in Encyclopedia or Reference Work

Oliver, Paul, and Barry Kernfeld. "Blues." <u>The New Grove</u>

<u>Dictionary of Jazz</u>. Ed. Barry Kernfeld. New York: St.

Martin's, 1994.

"The History of Western Theatre." <u>The New Encyclopaedia</u>

<u>Britannica: Macropedia</u>. 15th ed. 1987. Vol. 28.

11b
MLA

34. Chapter in Edited Book or Selection in Anthology

```
Atwood, Margaret. "Bluebeard's Egg." "Bluebeard's Egg" and
     Other Stories. New York: Fawcett-Random, 1987. 131-64.
```

For a reprinted selection, also identify the original source.

```
Atwood, Margaret. "Bluebeard's Egg." "Bluebeard's Egg" and
     Other Stories. New York: Fawcett-Random, 1987. 131-64.
     Rpt. in Don't Bet on the Prince: Contemporary Feminist
     Fairy Tales in North America and England. Ed. Jack Zipes.
     New York: Methuen, 1986. 160-82.
```

35. More Than One Selection from Anthology or Collection

Include an entry for the collection and the author's name as a basis for cross-references.

```
Goldberg, Jonathan. "Speculation: Macbeth and Source." Howard
     and O'Connor 242-64.

Howard, Jean E., and Marion F. O'Connor, eds. Shakespeare
     Reproduced: The Text in History and Ideology. New York:
     Methuen, 1987.
```

36. Preface, Foreword, Introduction, or Afterword

```
Tomlin, Janice. Foreword. The Complete Guide to Foreign
     Adoption. By Barbara Brooke Bascom and Carole A. McKelvey.
     New York: Pocket, 1997.
```

37. Letter (Published)

Garland, Hamlin. "To Fred Lewis Pattee." 30 Dec. 1914. Letter
206 of <u>Selected Letters of Hamlin Garland</u>. Ed. Keith Newlin
and Joseph B. McCullough. Lincoln: U of Nebraska P, 1998.

38. Dissertation Abstract

Hawkins, Joanne Berning. "Horror Cinema and the Avante-Garde."
Diss. U. of California, Berkeley, 1993. <u>DAI</u> 55 (1995):
1712A.

Field and Media Resources

39. Interview (Unpublished)

Schutt, Robin. Personal interview. 7 Oct. 2001.

Coppola, Francis Ford. Interview with James Lipton. <u>Inside the</u>
<u>Actors Studio</u>. Bravo, New York. 10 July 2001.

40. Survey or Questionnaire

MLA does not specify a form for these field resources. When citing your
own field research, you may wish to use the following format.

Figliozzi, Jennifer Emily, and Summer J. Arrigo-Nelson.
Questionnaire on Student Alcohol Use and Parental Values.
University of Rhode Island, Kingston. 15-20 Apr. 1998.

41. Observation

MLA does not specify a form for this type of field research. You may wish
to use the following form to cite your notes on field observations.

Ba, Ed. Ski Run Observation. Vail, CO. 26 Jan. 2002.

42. Letter or Memo (Unpublished)

Hall, Donald. Letter to the author. 24 Jan. 1990.

43. Oral Presentation

Shields, Carolyn. "Can Perrogies, Potlatches, and Polkas Combat
    Racism?" Leadership in Culturally Diverse Schools. Amer.
    Educ. Research Assn. Sheraton Hotel, New Orleans. 27 Apr.
    2000.

44. Performance

Cabaret. By Joe Masteroff. Dir. Sam Mendes. Studio 54, New
    York. 2 July 2001.

45. Videotape or Film

Rosencrantz and Guildenstern Are Dead. Dir. Tom Stoppard. Perf.
    Gary Oldman, Tim Roth, and Richard Dreyfuss.
    Videocassette. Buena Vista Home Video, 1990.
Rosencrantz and Guildenstern Are Dead. Dir. Tom Stoppard. Perf.
    Gary Oldman, Tim Roth, and Richard Dreyfuss. Cinecom
    Entertainment, 1990.

46. Television or Radio Program

"The Tour." I Love Lucy. Dir. William Asher. Nickelodeon.
    2 July 2001.

47. Recording

The Goo-Goo Dolls. Dizzy Up the Girl. Warner, 1998.

Mozart, Wolfgang Amadeus. Symphony no. 40 in G minor. Vienna

>   Philharmonic. Cond. Leonard Bernstein. Audiocassette.

>   Deutsche Grammophon, 1984.

48. Artwork or Photograph

Leonardo da Vinci. Mona Lisa. Louvre, Paris.

49. Map or Chart

Arkansas. Map. Comfort, TX: Gousha, 1996.

50. Cartoon

Cochran, Tony. "Agnes." Cartoon. Denver Post 10 June 1999: 10E.

51. Advertisement

Toyota. Advertisement. GQ July 2001: 8.

Internet, Web, and Electronic Resources

For each entry supply both the date when the material was posted (or last revised or updated) and then the date you accessed it. Note the complete address or URL (beginning with *http, gopher, telnet, ftp*) in angle brackets. Include the links, path, or file name needed for a reader to reach the page or frame you used. Break the line only after a slash (without adding a hyphen).

52. Professional Web Site

History of the American West, 1860-1920. 25 July 2000. Denver

>   Public Library. 16 Oct. 2001 <http://memory.loc.gov/ammem/

>   award97/codhtml>.

53. Individual Web Site

Baron, Dennis. Home page. 16 Aug. 2000. Dept. of English,

U of Illinois, Urbana-Champaign. 23 Aug. 2000

<http://www.english.uiuc.edu/baron/index.htm>.

54. Online Book

London, Jack. The Iron Heel. New York: Macmillan, 1908. The

Jack London Collection. 10 Dec. 1999. Berkeley Digital

Library SunSITE. 15 July 2001 <http://sunsite.berkeley.edu/

London/Writing/IronHeel/>.

55. Selection from Online Book

Muir, John. "The City of the Saints." Steep Trails. 1918. 17

July 2001 <http://encyclopediaindex.com/b/sttrl10.htm>.

56. Online Journal Article

Dugdale, Timothy. "The Fan and (Auto)Biography: Writing the

Self in the Stars." Journal of Mundane Behavior 1.2

(2000). 19 Sept. 2000 <http://www.mundanebehavior.org/

issues/v1n2/dugdale.htm>.

57. Online Magazine Article

Rickford, John R. "Suite for Ebony and Phonics." Discover Dec.

1997. 15 Aug. 2000 <http://www.discover.com/archive/

index.html>.

58. Online Newspaper or News Service Article

Mulvihill, Kim. "Childhood Obesity." San Francisco Chronicle 12

July 2001. 15 July 2001 <http://www.sfgate.com/cgi-bin/

article.cgi?file=/kron/archive/2001/07/12/obesity.DTL>.

59. Online Government Document

United States. Dept. of Commerce. Bureau of the Census. Census

Brief: Disabilities Affect One-Fifth of All Americans.

Dec. 1997. 18 July 2001 <http://www.census.gov/prod/3/

97pubs/cenbr975.pdf>.

60. Online Editorial

Ely, Jane. "For the Young, Get Houston the Games." Editorial.

Houston Chronicle 17 July 2001. 17 July 2001

<http://www.chron.com/cs/CDA/story.hts/editorial/970112>.

61. Online Letter to the Editor

Hadjiargyrou, Michael. "Stem Cells and Delicate Questions."

Letter. New York Times on the Web 17 July 2001. 18 July

2001 <http://www.nytimes.com/2001/07/18/opinion/

L18STEM.html>.

62. Online Interview

Rikker, David. Interview with Victor Payan. San Diego Latino

Film Festival. 1999. 20 Jan. 2002 <http://

www.sdlatinofilm.com/video.html#Anchor-David-64709>.

11b
MLA

63. Online Review

Chaudhury, Parama. Rev. of <u>Kandahar</u>, dir. Mohsen

    Makhmalbaf. <u>Film Monthly</u> 3.14 (2002). 19 Jan. 2002.

    <http://www.filmmonthly.com/Playing/Articles/Kandahar/

    Kandahar.html>.

64. Online Database, Information Service, or Scholarly Project

<u>The On-Line Books Page Presents Banned Books On-Line</u>. Ed. John

    Mark Ockerbloom. 7 Feb. 1999 <http://www.cs.cmu.edu/

    People/spok/banned-books.html>.

65. Online Source from Computer Service

"Native American Food Guide." <u>Healthfinder</u>. 16 July 2001.

    America Online. 16 July 2001. Keyword: Health.

66. Online Abstract

Prelow, Hazel, and Charles A. Guarnaccia. "Ethnic and Racial

    Differences in Life Stress among High School Adolescents."

    <u>Journal of Counseling & Development</u> 75.6 (1997). Abstract.

    6 Apr. 1998 <http://www.counseling.org/journals/

    jcdjul197.htm#Prelow>.

67. Online Videotape or Film

Coppola, Francis Ford, dir. <u>Apocalypse Now</u>. 1979.

    <u>Film.com</u>. 17 July 2001 <http://ramhurl.film.com/

    smildemohurl.ram?file=screen/2001/clips/apoca.smi>.

68. Online Television or Radio Program

Edwards, Bob. "Adoption: Redefining Family." <u>Morning Edition</u>.

Natl. Public Radio. 28-29 June 2001. 17 July 2001

<http://www.npr.org/programs/morning/features/2001/jun/

010628.cfoa.html>.

69. Online Recording

Malcolm X. "The Definition of Black Power." 8 Mar. 1964. <u>Great

Speeches</u>. 2000. 18 July 2001 <http://www.chicago-law.net/

speeches/speech.html#1m>.

70. Online Artwork

<u>Elamite Goddess</u>. 2100 BC (?). Louvre, Paris. 16 July 2001

<http://www.louvre.fr/louvrea.htm>.

71. Online Map or Chart

"Beirut [Beyrout] 1912." Map. <u>Perry-Castañeda Library Map

Collection</u>. 16 July 2000 <http://www.lib.utexas.edu/maps/

historical/beirut2_1912.jpg>.

72. Online Cartoon

Auth, Tony. "Spending Goals." Cartoon. <u>Slate</u> 7 Sept. 2001. 16

Oct. 2001 <http://cagle.slate.msn.com/politicalcartoons/

pccartoons/archives/auth.asp>.

73. Online Advertisement

```
Mazda Miata. Advertisement. 16 July 2001 <http://

    www.mazdausa.com/miata/>.
```

74. Other Electronic Sources

When citing an electronic source not explained above, adapt the appropriate nonelectronic MLA model. Include the date of access and electronic address.

```
NASA/JPL. "Martian Meteorite." Views of the Solar System:

    Meteoroids and Meteorites. Ed. Calvin J. Hamilton.

    1999. 13 June 1999 <http://spaceart.com/solar/eng/

    meteor.htm#views>.
```

75. FTP, Telnet, or Gopher Site

For sources obtained through FTP (file transfer protocol), telnet, or gopher, supply the address and other details as you would for a similar Web source.

11b
MLA

```
Lewis, Deanna L., and Ron Chepesuik. "The International Trade

    in Toxic Waste: A Selected Bibliography." Electronic Green

    Journal 1.2 (1994). 29 Apr. 1996 <ftp.uiadaho.edupub/

    docs/pub/publications/EGJ>.
```

76. Email

Give the writer's name, the title (or type) of communication, and the date.

```
Trimbur, John. E-mail to the author. 17 Sept. 2000.
```

77. Online Posting

Aid readers (if you can) by citing a stored version.

```
Brock, Stephen E. "School Crisis." Online posting. 27 Apr.

    2001. Special Events Chat Transcripts. Lycos Communities.

    18 July 2001 <http://clubs.lycos.com/live/Events/

    transcripts/school_crisis_tscript.asp>.
```

78. Synchronous Communication

When citing material from a MUD, MOO, or other form of synchronous communication, identify the speaker, the event, its date, its forum (such as CollegeTownMOO), and your access date. End with *telnet* and the address. Cite an archived version if possible.

```
Finch, Jeremy. Online debate "Can Proust Save Your

    Life?" 3 Apr. 1998. CollegeTownMOO. 3 Apr. 1998

    <telnet://next.cs.bvc.edu.7777>.
```

79. CD-ROM, Diskette, or Magnetic Tape

```
Shakespeare, William. All's Well That Ends Well. William

    Shakespeare: The Complete Works on CD-ROM. CD-ROM.

    Abingdon, Eng.: Andromeda Interactive, 1994.
```

80. CD-ROM Abstract

```
Blich, Baruch. "Pictorial Representation and Its Cognitive

    Status." Visual Arts Research 15 (1989): 68-75. Abstract.

    PsycLIT. CD-ROM. SilverPlatter. 3 Mar. 1996.
```

11c   MLA sample pages

The *MLA Handbook* recommends beginning a research paper with the first page of the text, using the format shown on Kimlee Cunningham's first page.

11c
MLA

Kimlee Cunningham   **Heading without title page**   **1" margin
on each
side**
Professor N. Reynolds
                              Double-spaced heading and paper
English 201

5 May 1999

**¶ indented
5 spaces**   Disney's Magic Mirror Reflects Traditions of Old

1   Since Disney Studio's first animated feature, <u>Snow White and
the Seven Dwarfs</u> (1937), the portrayal of female characters has
changed in some obvious ways but has also remained the same in
some key respects. By contrasting <u>Snow White and the Seven Dwarfs</u>
with the recent animated features <u>Beauty and the Beast</u> (1991) and
<u>Aladdin</u> (1992), we can see the leading female characters becoming
more independent and assertive. At the same time, a comparison of
the three movies reveals the studio's continuing appeal to its
audiences' sense of feminine physical beauty.

2   It is probably an exaggeration to say that a character like
Belle in <u>Beauty and the Beast</u> is a lot like a contemporary
feminist, as one critic suggests (Showalter). However, we should
not simply ignore an interpretation like this. Even if many
people view a film like <u>Beauty and the Beast</u> (or <u>Aladdin</u>) as a
simple love story (Hoffman), the films nonetheless grow out of

the complicated values and roles that shape relationships today. Disney's contemporary portrayal of women characters shows a willingness to change with the times but also a reluctance to abandon traditional values and stereotypes.

3   Nearly sixty years separate Snow White and the Seven Dwarfs from Beauty and the Beast and Aladdin. During this time of great social change, the roles of women have expanded. The shift has been from American women as housewives to American women as workers, college students, and corporate executives. By contrasting the main female character in Snow White with those in Beauty and Aladdin, we can see that they reflect their own times and the social changes separating the different time periods.

[Paper continues, analyzing each character.]

11c
MLA

11c
MLA

Sources listed alphabetically

↕ 1" from top of page

↑ 1/2" from top
Cunningham 7
Page numbers continue

Heading centered   Works Cited

Aladdin. 1992. Videocassette. Walt Disney Company, 1993.

Allan, Robin. "Fifty Years of Snow White." *Journal of Popular Film and Television* 24 (1988): 155-63.

Baudrillard, Jean. "Disneyworld Company." Trans. Francois Debrix. *CTHEORY* 27 Mar. 1996. 20 Jan. 1999 <http://www.ctheory.com/e25-disneyworld_comp.html>.

Beauty and the Beast. 1991. Videocassette. Walt Disney Company, 1991.

Hoffman, Loreen. "Feminism in a Disney Film." Online posting. 2 Feb. 1998. 26 Aug. 1998 <wysiwyg://22/http://faculty.ucr.edu/wcb/s. . .t/master/2/forums/forum2/messages/7.htm>.

McKenna, M. A. J. "Film Provides 'Beauty'-ful Role Models." *Boston Herald* 1 Dec. 1991: A13+.

Rosenberg, Scott. "The Genie-us of Aladdin." *San Francisco Examiner* 25 Nov. 1992: B2.

Showalter, Elaine. "Beauty and the Beast: Disney Meets Feminism in a Liberated Love Story for the '90s." *Premiere* Oct. 1997: 66.

Snow White and the Seven Dwarfs. 1937. Videocassette. Walt Disney Company, 1994.

Additional lines indented 5 spaces

GUIDE TO APA FORMATS

APA Formats for In-Text (Parenthetical) Citations

APA Formats for References

**12
APA**

continued

12 APA

12 | APA Style

The APA (American Psychological Association) documentation style uses the author's name and the date of publication—within parentheses or the text—to identify a source. This in-text citation guides readers to a detailed entry in a reference list at the end of the paper.

Use this "name-and-date" style when you write in a social science field or in a workplace or public setting where readers prefer a name-and-date system or want to see immediately how current your sources are.

For more information on APA style, consult the *Publication Manual of the American Psychological Association* (5th ed., Washington, DC: APA, 2001) or updates posted on the APA Web site: <http://www.apastyle.org>.

12a APA in-text (parenthetical) citations

In the APA system, you generally use parentheses in the text to enclose references to your sources, noting author and date, separated by a comma. You may also mention the author's name in your discussion instead of the citation.

1. Author's Name in Parentheses

WITHIN PARENTHESES   One study of news directors at radio stations has examined annual salaries by gender (Cramer, 1993).

2. Author's Name in Discussion

PART OF DISCUSSION   As Cramer (1993) observes, salary differences by gender may not occur in all news roles.

3. Specific Reference

To specify the location of a quotation, paraphrase, summary, or other information, add a comma, *p.* or *pp.*, and then the page or pages in the source.

QUOTATION   The study finds that "women radio news directors have exceeded the men in yearly salary" (Cramer, 1993, p. 161).

For classical works, indicate the part of the work you are citing (chap. 5), not the page. Spell any potentially confusing words and the word *figure* (but use *para.* or ¶ for a paragraph in an electronic source).

4. One Author

You can vary your in-text citations by presenting the name in the text, both the name and date in parentheses, or both in the text.

Mallory's 1999 study of magnet schools confirmed trends identified earlier (Jacobson, 1989) and updated by Bailey (1996).

12a
APA

5. Two Authors

Include both names. Separate them with an ampersand (&) in parenthetical citations; in your text, use *and*.

```
Given evidence that married men earn more than unmarried men

(Chun & Lee, 2001), Nakosteen and Zimmer (2001) investigate

how earnings affect spousal selection.
```

6. Three to Five Authors

For the first citation, include all the names, separated by commas with *and* in the text or an ampersand (&) in parentheses.

```
Sadeh, Raviv, and Gruber (2000) related "sleep problems

and neuropsychological functioning in children"

(p. 292).
```

In following references, use the first author's name with *et al.* ("and others"): Sadeh et al. (2000) reported their findings.

7. Six or More Authors

In text citations, follow the first author's name with *et al.* (Berg et al., 1998). (See Entry 2 on p. 85.)

8. Corporate or Group Author

Spell out the name of the association, corporation, or government agency in the first citation. Follow any cumbersome name with an abbreviation in brackets so you can use the shorter form in later citations.

FIRST CITATION   Besides instilling fear, hate crimes limit where women live and work (National Organization of Women [NOW], 2001).

LATER CITATION   Pending legislation would strengthen the statutes on bias-motivated crimes (NOW, 2001).

12a
APA

9. No Author Given

Give the title or the first few words of a long title.

> These photographs represent people from all walks of life
>
> (*Friendship*, 2001).

Full title: *Friendship: Celebration of humanity*.

10. Work Cited More Than Once

When you cite the same source more than once in a paragraph, repeat the citation as necessary to clarify a page reference or specify one of several sources. If a second reference is clear, don't repeat the date.

> Much of the increase in personal debt can be linked to
>
> unrestrained use of credit cards (Schor, 1998, p. 73). In
>
> fact, according to Schor, roughly a third of consumers
>
> "describe themselves as either heavily or moderately in
>
> financial debt" (p. 72).

11. Authors with the Same Name

When your sources include authors with the same last name, use the authors' initials.

> Scholars have examined the development of African American
>
> culture during slavery and reconstruction (E. Foner, 1988),
>
> including the role of Frederick Douglass in this process
>
> (P. Foner, 1950).

**12a
APA**

12. Personal Communications, Including Interviews and Email

Cite letters, memos, interviews, email, telephone conversations, and similar sources using the person's name, the phrase *personal communication*, and the full date. Omit these sources from your reference list.

```
According to J. M. Hostos, the state no longer funds

services duplicated by county agencies (personal

communication, October 7, 2001).
```

13. Two or More Sources in a Citation

If you sum up information from several sources, list them all in your citation. Arrange them alphabetically, then oldest to most recent for works by the same author. Separate the authors with semicolons.

```
Several studies have related work performance and

personality (Furnham, 1992; Gilmer, 1961, 1977).
```

14. Two or More Works by the Same Author in the Same Year

If you use works published in the same year by the same author or author team, alphabetize the works and add letters after the year to distinguish them.

```
Gould (1987a, p. 73) makes a similar point.
```

15. Content Footnote

You may use a content footnote to expand material. In the text add a superscript number, placed slightly above the related line of text. Number notes consecutively. On a separate page at the end, below the centered heading "Footnotes," present the notes in numerical order, as in the text. Begin each with its superscript number. Indent a half inch (five to seven spaces) for the initial line in each note, and double-space all notes.

TEXT
```
I tape-recorded and transcribed all interviews.1
```

NOTES
```
      1Although background noise obscured some parts

of the tapes, these gaps did not substantially

affect the material studied.
```

12b APA reference list

Your list of sources enables readers to identify and consult the sources you have cited.

- Begin the list with the centered title "References" on a separate page at the end of your text but before appendixes or notes. (See pp. 101–102 for a sample list.)
- List your sources alphabetically by author (or title if there is no author), then oldest to most recent for those by the same author.
- Do not indent the first line of each entry; indent the rest like paragraphs, a half inch or five to seven spaces.
- Double-space the entire list. Leave a single space after a period in an entry (except in abbreviations such as U.S.).

Books and Works Treated as Books

Include the following information for books, pamphlets, and similar sources: last name of each author followed by a comma and the *initials only* of the first and middle names; year of publication in parentheses; title (capitalizing only the first word, the first word of a subtitle, and any proper names); city of publication (with the country or the state's postal abbreviation except for major cities); and publisher's name, without words such as *Inc.* or *Publishers*.

1. One Author

Wilson, W. J. (1996). *When work disappears: The world of the*

new urban poor. New York, Knopf.

2. Two or More Authors

List up to six authors; add *et al.* to indicate any others.

Biber, D., Conrad, S., & Reppen, R. (1998). *Corpus linguistics:*

Investigating language structure and use. Cambridge,

England: Cambridge University Press.

3. Corporate or Group Author

Treat the group as author. When author and publisher are the same, use *Author* after the place instead of repeating the name.

Amnesty International. (2001). *Annual report 2001* [Brochure].

London: Author.

4. No Author Given

Boas anniversary volume: Anthropological papers written in

honor of Franz Boas. (1906). New York: Stechert.

5. More Than One Work by the Same Author

List works chronologically.

Aronowitz, S. (1993). *Roll over Beethoven: The return of*

cultural strife. Hanover, NH: Wesleyan University Press.

Aronowitz, S. (2000). *From the ashes of the old: American*

labor and America's future. New York: Basic Books.

6. More Than One Work by the Same Author in the Same Year

Gould, S. J. (1987a). *Time's arrow, time's cycle: Myth and*

metaphor in the discovery of geological time. Cambridge,

MA: Harvard University Press.

Gould, S. J. (1987b). *An urchin in the storm: Essays about*

books and ideas. New York: Norton.

7. One or More Editors

Bowe, J., Bowe, M., & Streeter, S. C. (Eds.). (2001). *Gig:*

Americans talk about their jobs. New York: Three Rivers

Press.

12b
APA

8. Translator

Bourdieu, P. (1990). *In other words: Essays towards a reflexive sociology* (M. Adamson, Trans.). Stanford, CA: Stanford University Press.

9. Edition Following the First

Groth-Marnat, G. (1996). *Handbook of psychological assessment* (3rd ed.). New York: Wiley.

10. Reprint

Butler, J. (1999). *Gender trouble*. New York: Routledge. (Original work published 1990)

11. Multivolume Work

Strachey, J., Freud, A., Strachey, A., & Tyson, A. (Eds.). (1966-1974). *The standard edition of the complete psychological works of Sigmund Freud* (J. Strachey et al., Trans.) (Vols. 3-5). London: Hogarth Press and the Institute of Psycho-Analysis.

12b
APA

12. Anthology or Collection of Articles

Cobley, P. (Ed.). (1996). *The communication theory reader*. London: Routledge.

13. Encyclopedia or Reference Work

Winn, P. (Ed.). (2001). *Dictionary of biological psychology*. London: Routledge.

14. *Diagnostic and Statistical Manual of Mental Disorders*

After an initial full in-text citation for this widely cited manual, use these abbreviations: *DSM-III* (1980), *DSM-III-R* (1987), *DSM-IV* (1994), or *DSM-IV-TR* (2000).

American Psychiatric Association. (1994). *Diagnostic and*

statistical manual of mental disorders (4th ed.).

Washington, DC: Author.

15. Dissertation (Unpublished)

Gomes, C. S. (2001). *Selection and treatment effects in*

managed care. Unpublished doctoral dissertation, Boston

University.

16. Government Document

Select Committee on Aging, Subcommittee on Human Services,

House of Representatives. (1991). *Grandparents' rights:*

Preserving generational bonds (Com. Rep. No. 102-833).

Washington, DC: U.S. Government Printing Office.

17. Report

Dossey, J. A. (1988). *Mathematics: Are we measuring up?* (Report

No. 17-M-02). Princeton, NJ: Educational Testing Service.

(ERIC Document Reproduction Service No. ED300207)

Articles and Selections from Periodicals and Books

For an article, provide the following information: author's name (last name first); date (in parentheses); title (without quotation marks, capitalizing only the first word of the main title and any subtitle or proper names); journal title (in italics, capitalizing all main words), volume number (in italics), and page numbers.

18. Article in Journal Paginated by Volume

Macklin, M. C. (1996). Preschoolers' learning of brand names

from visual cues. *Journal of Consumer Research, 23,* 251-

261.

19. Article in Journal Paginated by Issue

Sadeh, A., Raviv, A., & Gruber, R. (2000). Sleep patterns and

sleep disruptions in school-age children. *Developmental*

Psychology, 36(3), 291-301.

20. Special Issue of Journal

Balk, D. E. (Ed.). (1991). Death and adolescent bereavement

[Special issue]. *Journal of Adolescent Research, 6*(1).

21. Article in Weekly Magazine

Adler, J. (1995, July 31). The rise of the overclass. *Newsweek,*

126, 33-34, 39-40, 43, 45-46.

22. Article in Monthly Magazine

Dold, C. (1998, September). Needles and nerves. *Discover, 19,*

59-62.

23. Article with No Author Given

True tales of false memories. (1993, July/August). *Psychology*

Today, 26, 11-12.

24. Article in Newspaper

Murtaugh, P. (1998, August 10). Finding a brand's real essence.

Advertising Age, p. 12.

25. Editorial or Letter to the Editor

Ellis, S. (2001, September 7). Adults are problem with youth

sports [Letter to the editor]. *USA Today*, p. 14A.

26. Interview (Published)

Although APA does not specify a form for published interviews, you may wish to employ the following form.

Dess, N. K. (2001). The new body-mind connection (John T.

Cacioppo) [Interview]. *Psychology Today, 34*(4), 30-31.

27. Review with Title

McMahon, R. J. (2000). The Pentagon's war, the media's war

[Review of the book *Reporting Vietnam: Media and military

at war*]. *Reviews in American History, 28*, 303-308.

28. Review Without Title

Van Meter, E. J. (1994). [Review of the book *Preparing

tomorrow's school leaders: Alternative designs*].

Educational Administration Quarterly, 30, 112-117.

29. Article in Encyclopedia or Reference Work

Chernoff, H. (1978). Decision theory. In *International

encyclopedia of statistics* (Vol. 1, pp. 131-135). New

York: Free Press.

30. Chapter in Edited Book or Selection in Anthology

Chisholm, J. S. (1999). Steps to an evolutionary ecology of

mind. In A. L. Hinton (Ed.), *Biocultural approaches to the*

emotions (pp. 117-150). Cambridge, England: Cambridge

University Press.

31. Dissertation Abstract

Yamada, H. (1989). American and Japanese topic management

strategies in business conversations. *Dissertation*

Abstracts International, 50(09), 2982B.

Field and Media Resources

32. Unpublished Raw Data

Briefly describe the topic of data from field research in brackets; end with *Unpublished raw data.*

Hernandez, J. (1998). [Survey of attitudes on unemployment

benefits]. Unpublished raw data.

33. Interview (Unpublished)

Cite an interview you have conducted only in the text. (See Entry 12 on pp. 83–84.)

34. Personal Communications (Including Email)

Cite letters, email, phone calls, and other communications that cannot be consulted by your readers only in the text. (See Entry 12 on pp. 83–84.)

35. Paper Presented at a Meeting

Nelson, J. S. (1993, August). *Political argument in political*

science: A meditation on the disappointment of political

12b
APA

theory. Paper presented at the annual meeting of the
American Political Science Association, Chicago.

36. Videotape or Film

Musen, K. (Producer/Writer), & Zimbardo, P. (Writer). (1990).
Quiet rage: The Stanford prison study [Motion picture].
(Available from Insight Media, New York)

37. Television or Radio Program

Siceloff, J. L. (Executive Producer). (2002). *Now with Bill
Moyers* [Television series]. New York: WNET.

38. Recording

Freeman, R. (1994). Porscha [Recorded by R. Freeman & The
Rippingtons]. On *Sahara* [CD]. New York: GRP Records.

Internet, Web, and Electronic Resources

39. Web Site

12b
APA

Brown, D. K. (1998, April 1). *The children's literature web
guide*. Calgary: Author. Retrieved August 23, 1998, from
http://www.acs.UCalgary.ca/~dkbrown/

40. Online Book or Document

If you can't find a publication date, use *n.d.* ("no date").

Frary, R. B. (n.d.). *A brief guide to questionnaire
development*. Retrieved August 8, 1998, from
http://ericae.net/ft/ tamu/upiques3.htm

41. Selection from Online Book or Document

Lasswell, H. D. (1971). Professional training. In *A*

pre-view of policy sciences (chap. 8). Retrieved

May 4, 2002, from http://www.policysciences.org/

spsresources.htm

42. Online Journal Article

Sheridan, J., & McAuley, J. D. (1998). Rhythm as a cognitive

skill: Temporal processing deficits in autism. *Noetica,*

3(8). Retrieved December 31, 1998, from http://www.cs

.indiana.edu/Noetica/OpenForumIssue8/McAuley.html

43. Online Article Identical to Print Version

If online and print articles are identical, you may use the print format but identify the online version you used.

Epstein, R. (2001). Physiologist Laura [Electronic version].

Psychology Today, 34(4), 5.

If the online article differs in format or content, add your retrieval date with the URL.

44. Online Newsletter Article

Cashel, J. (2001, July 16). Top ten trends for online

communities. *Online Community Report*. Retrieved October

18, 2001, from http://www.onlinecommunityreport.com/

features/10/

12b
APA

45. Online Newspaper or News Service Article

Phillips, D. (1999, June 13). 21 days, 18 flights. *Washington Post Online*. Retrieved June 13, 1999, from http://www.washingtonpost.com/wp-srv/business/daily/june99/odyssey13.htm

46. Online Organization or Agency Document

Arizona Public Health Association. (n.d.). *Indigenous health section*. Retrieved September 6, 2001, from http://www.geocities.com/native_health_az/AzPHA.htm

47. Online Government Document

U.S. Department of Labor, Women's Bureau. (2001). *Women's jobs 1964-1999: More than 30 years of progress*. Retrieved September 7, 2001, from http://www.dol.gov/dol/wb/public/jobs6497.htm

48. Online Document from Academic Site

Cultural Studies Program. (n.d.). Retrieved September 9, 2001, from Drake University, Cultural Studies Web site: http://www.multimedia.drake.edu/cs/

49. Online Report

Amnesty International. (1998). *The death penalty in Texas: Lethal injustice*. Retrieved September 7, 2001, from http://www.web.amnesty.org/ai.nsf/index/AMR510101998

50. Online Report from Academic Site

Use "Available from" rather than "Retrieved from" if the URL will take your reader to access information rather than the source itself.

Vandell, D. L., & Wolfe, B. (2000). *Child care quality:*

Does it matter and does it need to be improved?

(Special Report No. 78). Available from University of

Wisconsin, Institute for Research on Poverty Web site:

http://www.ssc.wisc.edu/irp/sr/sr78.pdf

51. Online Abstract

National Bureau of Economic Research. (1998). Tax incentives

for higher education. *Tax Policy and the Economy,*

12, 49-81. Abstract retrieved August 24, 1998, from

http://www-mitpress.mit.edu/journal-editor

.tcl?ISSN=08928649

52. Journal Article from Online Database

Piko, B. (2001). Gender differences and similarities in

adolescents' ways of coping. *Psychological Record, 51*(2),

223-236. Retrieved August 31, 2001, from InfoTrac Expanded

Academic database.

53. Newspaper Article from Online Database

Li, R. J. (1999, May 4). Ohio State U. Greeks "aware" alcohol

not necessary for fun. *The Lantern*. Retrieved July 22,

1999, from Electric Library database.

12b
APA

54. Presentation from Virtual Conference

```
Brown, D. J., Stewart, D. S., & Wilson, J. R. (1995). Ethical
     pathways to virtual learning. Paper presented at the
     Center on Disabilities 1995 virtual conference. Retrieved
     September 7, 2001, from http://www.csun.edu/cod/
     95virt/0010.html
```

55. Email

Cite email only in your text. (See Entry 12, pp. 83–84.)

56. Online Posting

Treat these as personal communications (see Entry 12, pp. 83–84) unless they are archived and accessible.

```
Lanbehn, K. (2001, May 9). Effective rural outreach. Message
     posted to State Independent Living Council Discussion
     Newsgroup, archived at http://www.acils.com/silc/
```

57. Computer Program

Begin with the name of an author who owns rights to a program or with its title (without italics).

```
Family Tree Maker (Version 9.0) [Computer software]. (2001).
     Fremont, CA: Learning Company.
```

58. CD-ROM Database

```
Hall, Edward T. (1998). In Current biography: 1940-1997.
     Retrieved March 14, 1999, from Wilson database.
```

12c APA sample pages

The APA manual recommends beginning a research paper with a title page, using the format illustrated in the paper below. These student writers also included an abstract before the paper and their questionnaire in the appendix following it.

[New page]

**Number title page
and all others**   Alcohol Use   1
using short title

Running head: ALCOHOL USE   **Abbreviate title
(50 characters
maximum) for
heading**

**Center
title and
all other** Alcohol Use: Correlations Between College Drinking
lines
          and Previous Parental Permissiveness

Supply Jennifer Emily Figliozzi and Summer J. Arrigo-Nelson
**names and
institution**   The University of Rhode Island

12c
APA

          Professor Robert Schwegler   **Supply course
information**
          Writing 201   **and date if
requested**
          Section 1   **by your
instructor**
          May 1, 1998

[New page]

Abstract   **Center heading**

Do not indent College students at a medium-sized state university were asked to fill out a questionnaire on their parents' attitudes toward alcohol use and their own drinking behaviors. The study addressed two research questions: (a) Do students given permission to drink **Double-space abstract and paper** while still living at home exhibit different college drinking behaviors than those who were not given permission? and (b) Do students feel there is a correlation between college drinking behaviors and permission to drink while still living at home? The study found evidence both of a correlation between parental permission and drinking behaviors and of student belief that such a correlation exists.

Summari paper in one ¶, n more tha 120 wor

**12c
APA**

Besides the abstract, typical sections in an APA paper are Introduction, Method, Results, and Discussion

[New page]

↕ **1" from top of page**

Alcohol Use: Correlations Between College Drinking

and Previous Parental Permissiveness

Research dealing with student alcohol use most often focuses   **Indent ¶s consistently ½" or 5 to 7 spaces**
on children's perceptions of their parents' actions and on the
relationship between child and parent. Studies conducted with high
school students have supported the hypothesis that positive family
relationships are more likely to be associated with less frequent
alcohol use among adolescents than are negative relationships.   **1" margin on each side**
Adolescents model the limited substance use of their parents where
there is a good or moderate parent-adolescent relationship
(Andrews, Hops, & Duncan, 1997). Other factors the studies found
to be associated with positive family relationships, along with
substance use, were academic achievement, family structure, place
of residence, self-esteem, and emotional tone (Martsh & Miller,
1997; Wechsler, Dowdall, Davenport, & Castillo, 1995).

12c APA

Introduction   **Center subheading**

The focus of our study is twofold. First, research has shown
that adolescents who have open and close relationships with their

1" margin at bottom

parents use alcohol less often than do those with conflictual
relationships (Sieving, 1996). For example, a survey of students
in seventh through twelfth grades reported that approximately 35%
of adolescent drinkers were under parental supervision while
drinking (Department of Education, 1993). On the basis of this
research, we are interested in determining if students who were
given permission to drink while living with their parents would
have different drinking patterns upon reaching college than those
who did not previously have permission to drink.

　　　Second, studies have demonstrated that student perception of
parental drinking behavior and parental restrictiveness shapes
student behavior as much as, if not more than, actual parental
behavior (Aas, Jakobsen, & Anderssen, 1996). Considering this,
we are also interested in learning if students feel that a
correlation exists between having permission to drink at home and
their behavior once in college.

[Paper continues.]

12c
APA

[New page]

References

Aas, H., Jakobsen, R., & Anderssen, N. (1996). Predicting 13-
     year-olds' drinking using parents' self-reported alcohol use
     and restrictiveness compared with offspring's perception.
     Scandinavian Journal of Psychology, 37, 113-120.

Andrews, J. A., Hops, H., & Duncan, S. C. (1997). Adolescent
     modeling of parent substance use: The moderating effect of
     the relationship with the parent. *Journal of Family
     Psychology, 11,* 259-270.

Department of Education. (1993). *Youth and alcohol. Selected
     reports to the Surgeon General* (Report No. OESC-92-38).
     Washington, DC: Author. (ERIC Document Reproduction Service
     No. ED361616)

Martsh, C. T., & Miller, W. R. (1997). Extraversion predicts heavy
     drinking in college students. *Personality and Individual
     Differences, 23,* 153-155.

Sieving, R. E. (1996, Fall). Parental influence on alcohol use
     among young adolescents. *GSAN Newsletter.* Retrieved April 25,
     1998, from http://www.nursing.umn.edu/MS/Adolescent/
     Newsletter/fall1996.html

Do not indent first line

Indent each following line as you indent a ¶

**12c
APA**

Wechsler, H., Dowdall, G. W., Davenport, A., & Castillo, S.

   (1995). Correlates of college student binge drinking.

   American Journal of Public Health, 85, 921-926.

Wechsler, H., Dowdall, G. W., Davenport, A., & DeJong, W. (n.d.).

   Binge drinking on campus: Results of a national study.

   Bulletin Series: Alcohol and Other Drug Prevention. Newton,

   MA: The Higher Education Center for Alcohol and Other

   Drug Prevention. Retrieved April 29, 1998, from

   http://www.edc.org/hec/pubs/binge.htm

12c
APA

GUIDE TO CMS FORMATS

CMS Formats for Endnotes and Footnotes

CMS Formats for Bibliography Entries

13
CMS

continued

CMS Formats for Bibliography Entries (*continued*)

**Internet, Web, and
Electronic Resources**
20. Online Book
21. Online Article
22. CD-ROM

Multiple Sources
23. Multiple Sources

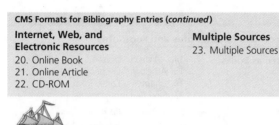

13 | CMS Style

The CMS (*Chicago Manual of Style*) outlines a system for references using endnotes or footnotes. These notes are less compact than parenthetical references but allow detailed citations. They work well when readers won't need to consult each note and might be distracted by information in parentheses. Use the CMS style in academic settings in the arts and sciences, such as history, or when an instructor requests "Turabian," "Chicago," or a footnote or endnote style.

The CMS style shown here is one of two documentation systems outlined in *The Chicago Manual of Style* (14th edition, Chicago: University of Chicago Press, 1993), often simply called "Chicago." Its Web site at <http://www.press.uchicago.edu/Misc/Chicago/cmosfaq.html> answers many questions for writers and editors who routinely use CMS. This style is detailed for students in Kate L. Turabian's *A Manual for Writers of Term Papers, Theses, and Dissertations* (6th ed., rev. John Grossman and Alice Bennett, Chicago: University of Chicago Press, 1996), known as "Turabian."

13a CMS notes

To indicate a reference in your text, insert a superscript number, which appears slightly above the line. Number all your references consecutively. Provide the note with the details about the source at the end of the paper (endnote) or at the bottom of the page (footnote). A typical note supplies the author's name in regular order, title, publication information, and page reference.

TEXT   Wideman describes his childhood neighborhood as being not simply on "the wrong side of the tracks" but actually "*under* the tracks."[1]

NOTE   1. John Edgar Wideman, *Brothers and Keepers* (New York: Penguin Books, 1984), 39.

Endnotes are generally easy to prepare (and easy for readers to consult), though some word processors can position footnotes between the text and the bottom margin. Place endnotes at the end of your paper, after any appendix but before the bibliography, which alphabetically orders your sources.

Supply the notes on a separate page with the centered heading "Notes." For each note, indent the first line like a paragraph. Start with the number, typed on the line and followed by a period and a space. Do not indent the lines that follow. CMS suggests double-spacing all parts of your text, but Turabian suggests single-spaced notes. We advise double-spacing for ease of reading.

Because readers may skip notes, put all essential material in your text, not in the notes. If you supply points of interest to only a few readers, avoid excessive, distracting detail.

13a
CMS

TEXT   Another potential source of misunderstanding comes from differences in the ways orders are given by men (directly) and women (indirectly, often as requests or questions).[2]

NOTE   2. Deborah Tannen, "How to Give Orders Like a Man," *New York Times Magazine*, 18 August 1994, 46. Tannen provides a balanced, detailed discussion of the ways men and women use language in *Talking from 9 to 5* (New York: William Morrow, 1994).

Books and Works Treated as Books

1. One Author

1. Iris Chang, *The Rape of Nanking: The Forgotten Holocaust of World War II* (New York: Basic Books, 1997), 83.

2. Two Authors

2. William H. Gerdts and Will South, *California Impressionism* (New York: Abbeville Press, 1998), 214.

3. Three Authors

3. Michael Wood, Bruce Cole, and Adelheid Gealt, *Art of the Western World* (New York: Summit Books, 1989), 206-10.

4. Four or More Authors

Follow the name of the first with *and others*. (Generally supply all the names in the bibliography entry.)

4. Anthony Slide and others, *The American Film Industry: A Historical Dictionary* (New York: Greenwood Press, 1986), 124.

13a
CMS

5. No Author Given

5. *The Great Utopia* (New York: Guggenheim Museum, 1992), 661.

6. One Editor

6. Valantasis, Richard, ed., *Religions of Late Antiquity in Practice* (Princeton: Princeton University Press, 2000), 266.

7. Two or More Editors

7. Cris Mazza, Jeffrey DeShell, and Elisabeth Sheffield, eds., *Chick-Lit 2: No Chick Vics* (Normal, Ill.: Black Ice Books, 1996), 173-86.

8. Author and Editor

8. Francis Bacon, *The New Organon,* ed. Lisa Jardine, trans. Michael Silverthorne (Cambridge: Cambridge University Press, 2000), 45.

9. Edition Following the First

9. John D. La Plante, *Asian Art,* 3d ed. (Dubuque, Iowa: Wm. C. Brown, 1992), 7.

10. Reprint

10. Patrick V. Kirch and Marshall Sahlins, *Anahulu: The Anthropology of History in the Kingdom of Hawaii* (University of Chicago Press, 1992; reprint, Chicago: University of Chicago Press, 1994), 104-5.

11. Multivolume Work

11. Sigmund Freud, *The Standard Edition of the Complete Psychological Works of Sigmund Freud,* trans. James Strachey (London: Hogarth Press, 1953), 11: 180.

13a
CMS

Articles and Selections from Periodicals and Books

12. Article in Journal Paginated by Volume

12. C. Anita Tarr, "'A Man Can Stand Up': Johnny Tremain and the Rebel Pose," *The Lion and the Unicorn: A Critical Journal of Children's Literature* 18 (1994): 181.

13. Article in Journal Paginated by Issue

13. Jose Pinera, "A Chilean Model for Russia," *Foreign Affairs* 79, no. 5 (2000): 62-73.

14. Article in Magazine

14. Joan W. Gandy, "Portrait of Natchez," *American Legacy,* fall 2000, 51-52.

15. Article in Newspaper

15. Janny Scott, "A Bull Market for Grant, A Bear Market for Lee," *New York Times,* 30 September 2000, sec. A, pp. 17, 19.

16. Chapter in Edited Book

16. Julie D'Acci, "Defining Women: The Case of *Cagney and Lacey,*" in *Private Screenings: Television and the Female Consumer,* ed. Lynn Spigel and Denise Mann (Minneapolis: University of Minnesota Press, 1992), 169.

17. Selection in Anthology

17. W. E. B. Du Bois, "The Call of Kansas," in *W. E. B. Du Bois: A Reader,* ed. David Levering Lewis (New York: Henry Holt, 1995), 173.

Field and Media Resources

18. Interview (Unpublished)

18. Suhar Teran, interview by author, transcript, Tempe, Ariz., 22 May 2000.

19. Audio or Video Recording

19. *James Baldwin,* prod. and dir. Karen Thorsen, 87 min., Resolution Inc./California Newsreel, 1990, videocassette.

Internet, Web, and Electronic Resources

Include all standard information. Add the medium in brackets, such as [database online]. Supply your access date, the URL, and the network: INTERNET.

20. Online Book

> 20. Charles Darwin, *On the Origin of Species by Means of Natural Selection, or the Preservation of Favoured Races in the Struggle for Life* [book online] (London: Down, Bromley, Kent, 1859 [cited 12 February 1999]); available from ftp://sailor.gutenberg.org/pub/gutenberg/etext98/otoos10.txt; INTERNET.

21. Online Article

> 21. Alfred Willis, "A Survey of Surviving Buildings of the Krotona Colony in Hollywood," *Architronic* 8, no. 1 (1999) [journal online] [cited 29 September 2000]; available from http://architronic.saed.kent.edu/; INTERNET.

22. CD-ROM

> 22. Rose, Mark, ed., "Elements of Theater," *The Norton Shakespeare Workshop CD-ROM.* Vers. 1.1. [CD-ROM] (New York: Norton Publishing, 1997).

Multiple Sources and Source Cited in Prior Notes

23. Multiple Sources

> 23. See Greil Marcus, *Mystery Train: Images of America in Rock 'n Roll Music* (New York: E. P. Dutton, 1975), 119; and Susan Orlean, "All Mixed Up," *New Yorker,* 22 June 1992, 90.

24. Work Cited More Than Once

In your first reference, provide full information. Later, provide only the author's last name, short title, and page.

> 24. Pinera, "Chilean," 63.

> 25. Wood, Cole, and Gealt, *Art,* 207.

13a
CMS

If two notes in a row refer to the same source, you may use the abbreviation *Ibid.* ("in the same place") for the second note. (Add a new page reference when the specific page is different.)

```
26. Tarr, "'A Man,'" 183.
27. Ibid.
28. Ibid., 186.
```

13b CMS bibliography

In addition to your notes, provide readers with an alphabetical list of your sources, titled "Selected Bibliography," "Works Cited," "References," or something similar. Place this list on a separate page at the end of your paper, and center the title two inches below the upper edge. Continue the page numbering used for the text. Although we show single-spaced entries below to save space, we recommend double-spacing so your bibliography is easy to read. (Consult your instructor.) Do not indent the first line, but indent each subsequent line one-half inch or five spaces. Alphabetize entries by the authors' last names or by the first word of the title (excluding *A, An,* and *The*) if the author is unknown.

Books and Works Treated as Books

1. One Author

Chang, Iris. *The Rape of Nanking: The Forgotten Holocaust of World War II.* New York: Basic Books, 1997.

2. Two Authors

Gerdts, William H., and Will South. *California Impressionism.* New York: Abbeville Press, 1998.

3. Three Authors

Wood, Michael, Bruce Cole, and Adelheid Gealt. *Art of the Western World.* New York: Summit Books, 1989.

4. Four or More Authors

Slide, Anthony, Val Almen Darez, Robert Gitt, and Susan Perez Prichard. *The American Film Industry: A Historical Dictionary.* New York: Greenwood Press, 1986.

5. No Author Given

The Great Utopia. New York: Guggenheim Museum, 1992.

6. One Editor

Valantasis, Richard, ed. *Religions of Late Antiquity in Practice.* Princeton: Princeton University Press, 2000.

7. Two or More Editors

Mazza, Cris, Jeffrey DeShell, and Elisabeth Sheffield, eds. *Chick-Lit 2: No Chick Vics.* Normal, Ill.: Black Ice Books, 1996.

8. Author and Editor

Bacon, Francis. *The New Organon.* Ed. Lisa Jardine, trans. Michael Silverthorne. Cambridge: Cambridge University Press, 2000.

13b
CMS

9. Edition Following the First

La Plante, John D. *Asian Art.* 3d ed. Dubuque, Iowa: Wm. C. Brown, 1992.

10. Reprint

Kirch, Patrick V., and Marshall Sahlins. *Anahulu: The Anthropology of History in the Kingdom of Hawaii.* University of Chicago Press, 1992. Reprint, Chicago: University of Chicago Press, 1994.

11. Multivolume Work

Freud, Sigmund. *The Standard Edition of the Complete Psychological Works of Sigmund Freud.* Translated by James Strachey. Vol. 11. London: Hogarth Press, 1953.

Articles and Selections from Periodicals and Books

12. Article in Journal Paginated by Volume

Tarr, Anita C. "'A Man Can Stand Up': Johnny Tremain and the Rebel Pose." *The Lion and the Unicorn: A Critical Journal of Children's Literature* 18 (1994): 178-89.

13. Article in Journal Paginated by Issue

Pinera, Jose. "A Chilean Model for Russia." *Foreign Affairs* 79, no. 5 (2000): 62-73.

14. Article in Magazine

Gandy, Joan W. "Portrait of Natchez." *American Legacy,* fall 2000, 51-52.

15. Article in Newspaper

Scott, Janny. "A Bull Market for Grant, A Bear Market for Lee." *New York Times,* 30 September 2000, sec. A, pp. 17, 19.

16. Chapter in Edited Book

D'Acci, Julia. "Defining Women: The Case of *Cagney and Lacey.*" In *Private Screenings: Television and the Female Consumer,* edited by Lynn Spigel and Denise Mann, 169-201. Minneapolis: University of Minnesota Press, 1992.

17. Selection in Anthology

Du Bois, W. E. B. "The Call of Kansas." In *W. E. B. Du Bois: A Reader,* edited by David Levering Lewis, 101-121. New York: Henry Holt, 1995.

Field and Media Resources

18. Interview (Unpublished)

Teran, Suhar. Interview by author. Transcript. Tempe, Ariz.,
    22 May 2000.

19. Audio or Video Recording

James Baldwin. Produced and directed by Karen Thorsen. 87 min.
    Resolution Inc./California Newsreel, 1990. Videocassette.

Internet, Web, and Electronic Resources

20. Online Book

Darwin, Charles. *On the Origin of Species by Means of Natural
    Selection, or the Preservation of Favoured Races in the
    Struggle for Life* [book online]. (London: Down, Bromley,
    Kent, 1859 [cited 12 February 1999]). Available from
    ftp://sailor.gutenberg.org/pub/gutenberg/etext98/
    otoos10.txt; INTERNET.

21. Online Article

Willis, Alfred. "A Survey of Surviving Buildings of the Krotona
    Colony in Hollywood." *Architronic* 8, no. 1 (1999) [journal
    online] [cited 29 September 2000]. Available from
    http://architronic.saed.kent.edu/; INTERNET.

13b
CMS

22. CD-ROM

Rose, Mark, ed. "Elements of Theater." *The Norton Shakespeare
    Workshop CD-ROM.* Vers. 1.1. [CD-ROM] New York: Norton
    Publishing, 1994.

Multiple Sources

23. Multiple Sources

When a note lists more than one source, include each one separately in
your bibliography.

GUIDE TO CSE FORMATS

CSE Formats for References

Books and Works Treated as Books
1. One Author
2. Two or More Authors
3. Corporate or Group Author
4. Editor
5. Translator
6. Conference Proceedings
7. Report

Articles and Selections from Periodicals and Books
8. Article in Journal Paginated by Volume
9. Article in Journal Paginated by Issue

10. Article with Corporate or Group Author
11. Entire Issue of Journal
12. Chapter in Edited Book or Selection in Anthology
13. Figure from Article

Internet, Web, and Electronic Resources
14. Patent from Database or Information Service
15. Online Article
16. Online Abstract
17. CD-ROM Abstract

14 | CSE Style

One common form of documentation in the natural and applied sciences is the style used by CSE (Council of Science Editors), formerly CBE (Council of Biology Editors). This guide advocates a simplified international scientific style and presents two options for documentation: a name-and-year and a number system.

Use CSE style in academic settings when you write in scientific or technical fields or your instructor requests "scientific documentation." Use it in engineering, too, modified to follow the style required in a particular journal or by your instructor. (See 14c.) Consider using the style in other settings when your readers work in scientific fields, expect current scientific sources, or prefer a name-and-year or number system.

CSE style tends to have more variations than the other styles, mainly because different scientific fields have different requirements. Check expectations with your instructor, your readers, or the publication using the style you are following. For more information, see *Scientific Style and Format: The CBE Manual for Authors, Editors, and Publishers* (6th ed., Cambridge, Eng.: Cambridge University Press, 1994). Updates are available at <http://www.councilscienceeditors.org>.

14a CSE in-text citations

Use one of two methods for CSE in-text references.

Name-and-year method. With this method, you include the author's name and the publication date in parentheses (unless mentioned in the text).

WITHIN
PARENTHESES
> Decreases in the use of lead, cadmium, and zinc have resulted in a "very large decrease in the large-scale pollution of the troposphere" (Boutron and others 1991, p 64).

PART OF
DISCUSSION
> Boutron and others (1991) found that decreases in the use of lead, cadmium, and zinc have resulted in a "very large decrease in the large-scale pollution of the troposphere" (p 64).

14a
CSE

Distinguish several works by the same author, all dated in a single year, by letters (*a, b, c*) after the date.

Number method. Instead of names, use numbers placed in parentheses in the text or superscript numbers raised above the line; list corresponding numbered works in your reference list.

> Decreases in the use of lead, cadmium, and zinc have reduced pollution in the troposphere (1).

Your first option is to number your in-text citations consecutively as they appear and to arrange them accordingly in the reference list. Your second is to alphabetize your references first, number them, and then use the corresponding number in your paper. Because only the number appears in your text, mention the author's name if it is important.

14b CSE reference list

You may use "References" or "Cited References" to head your list. For the name-and-year method, alphabetize the references by the last name of the main author, and then order works by the same author by date of publication, oldest first. Place the date after the author's name, followed by a period.

For the consecutive number method, arrange your sources in the same sequence in your reference list as in your paper. For the alphabetized number method, arrange your list alphabetically, and then number the entries. The examples below illustrate the number method.

Books and Works Treated as Books

1. One Author

End the entry with a book's total number of pages.

1. Bishop RH. Modern control systems analysis and design using MATLAB. Reading: Addison-Wesley; 1993. 239 p.

2. Two or More Authors

2. Freeman JM, Kelly MT, Freeman JB. The epilepsy diet treatment: an introduction to the ketogenic diet. New York: Demo, 1994. 180 p.

3. Corporate or Group Author

3. Intergovernmental Panel on Climate Change. Climate change 1995: the science of climate change. Cambridge: Cambridge University Press; 1996. 572 p.

4. Editor

4. Dolphin D, editor. Biomimetic chemistry. Washington:
    American Chemical Society; 1980. 437 p.

5. Translator

5. Jacob F. The logic of life: a history of heredity.
    Spillmann BE, translator. New York: Pantheon Books; 1982.
    348 p. Translation of: Logique du vivant.

6. Conference Proceedings

6. Witt I, editor. Protein C: biochemical and medical
    aspects. Proceedings of the International Workshop; 1984
    Jul 9-11; Titisee, Germany. Berlin: De Gruyter; 1985.
    195 p.

7. Report

7. Environmental Protection Agency (US) [EPA]. Guides to
    pollution prevention: the automotive repair industry.
    Washington: US EPA; 1991; 46 p. Available from: EPA Office
    of Research and Development; EPA/625/7-91/013.

14b
CSE

Articles and Selections from Periodicals and Books

8. Article in Journal Paginated by Volume

8. Yousef YA, Yu LL. Potential contamination of groundwater
    from Cu, Pb, and Zn in wet detention ponds receiving
    highway runoff. J Environ Sci Hlth 1992;27:1033-44.

9. Article in Journal Paginated by Issue

9. Boutron CF. Decrease in anthropogenic lead, cadmium and
    zinc in Greenland snows since the late 1960's. Nature
    1991;353(6340):153-5, 160.

10. Article with Corporate or Group Author

10. Derek Sims Associates. Why and how of acoustic testing. Environ Eng 1991;4(1):10-12.

11. Entire Issue of Journal

11. Savage A, editor. Proceedings of the workshop on the zoo-university connection: collaborative efforts in the conservation of endangered primates. Zoo Biol 1989;1(Suppl).

12. Chapter in Edited Book or Selection in Anthology

12. Moro M. Supply and conservation efforts for nonhuman primates. In: Gengozian N, Deinhardt F, editors. Marmosets in experimental medicine. Basel: S. Karger AG; 1978. p 37-40.

13. Figure from Article

13. Kanaori Y, Kawakami SI, Yairi K. Space-time distribution patterns of destructive earthquakes in the inner belt of central Japan. Engng Geol 1991;31(3-4):209-30 (p 216, table 1).

14b
CSE

Internet, Web, and Electronic Resources

CSE recommends following the National Library of Medicine formats for Internet sources, reflected here and available through the CSE Web site.

14. Patent from Database or Information Service

14. Collins FS, Drumm ML, Dawson DC, Wilkinson DJ, inventors. Method of testing potential cystic fibrosis treating compounds using cells in culture. US patent 5,434,086.

1995 Jul 18. Available from: Lexis/Nexis/Lexpat
library/ALL file.

15. Online Article

15. Grolmusz V. On the weak mod m representation of Boolean
     functions. Chi J Theor Comp Sci [Internet] 1995
     [cited 1996 May 3];100-5. Available from:
     http://www.csuchicago.edu/publication/cjtcs/
     articles/1995/2/contents.html

16. Online Abstract

16. Smithies O, Maeda N. Gene targeting approaches to complex
     genetic diseases: atherosclerosis and essential
     hypertension [abstract]. Proc Natl Acad Sci USA
     [Internet]. 1995 [cited 1996 Jan 21];92(12):5266-72.
     1 screen. Available from: Lexis/Medline/ABST.

17. CD-ROM Abstract

17. MacDonald R, Fleming MF, Barry KL. Risk factors associated
     with alcohol abuse in college students [abstract]. Am J
     Drug and Alc Abuse [CD-ROM];17:439-49. Available from:
     SilverPlatter File: PsycLIT Item: 79-13172.

14c
CSE

14c Variations in scientific and technical style

CSE is a flexible style, accommodating two major systems for in-text citations (the name-and-year method and the number method; see 14a) and
several systems for reference lists (alphabetical by author, consecutive
number by sequence in the discussion, and numbered in alphabetical
order; see 14b). Given these widely accepted variations, you may need
to figure out exactly what style your readers and research community
expect.

STRATEGY Adapt CSE style as needed to meet community expectations.

- Review the general CSE guidelines so that you are able to recognize the major alternative patterns.
- Follow any specific directions supplied by your instructor, advisor, or supervisor. Ask what's expected if you aren't sure how to proceed.
- Check any specific guidelines or style manuals in your specialized scientific, engineering, or technical field.
- Look for guidelines for authors in a recommended or respected journal. Check the front and back of the journal or the sponsoring organization's Web site for directions or examples. Modify any prepublication directions as necessary to fit the type of document you are preparing.
- Carefully examine any paper or journal article suggested as a pattern. Pay attention to how the in-text citations are presented, how the reference list is organized, and how the details are arranged in the reference list entries.
- Match your own paper against your guidelines or models. Edit your in-text citations so that they follow the pattern in your model. Order the entries in your reference list as your model does. Arrange the details for each reference in the same way, checking punctuation, capitalization, italics or underlining, and so forth.

SECTION 4
Writing Correctly

Voices from the Community

❝ Using good grammar is one mark of an educated person.
. . . Clear communication is our goal. ❞

H. Moody, *Grammar Terms—Invention of the Devil?*

15 | Fragments

If you write a group of words that masquerade as a sentence but are incomplete, you may irritate or mislead your readers and undermine your own authority as a writer.

PARTS MISSING   The insurance company processing the claim.

> **READER'S REACTION: Something is missing. What did it *do*?**

EDITED   The insurance company processing the claim **sent** a check.

Even with a capital letter at the beginning and a period at the end, a **sentence fragment** is only part of a sentence—it may lack a **subject** (naming the doer) or a **verb** (naming the action or occurrence). It may be a **subordinate clause,** introduced by a word like *because* and mistakenly asked to stand on its own.

15a Recognizing sentence fragments

Subject and verb. A **complete sentence** must contain both a subject and a complete verb, expressed or implied.

STRATEGY Ask questions to test sentences.

- Test #1: Ask *who* or *what does*? Or *Who* or *what is*?

A word group that doesn't answer "Who?" or "What?" lacks a subject and is a fragment. Especially if it begins with *and* or *but,* it may be detached from a nearby sentence with its subject.

FRAGMENT   And also needs a counselor.

> **READER'S REACTION: I can't tell *who* (or *what*) needs the counselor.**

EDITED   **Hope Clinic hired a nurse** and also needs a counselor.

A word group that doesn't answer "Does?" or "Is?" lacks a complete verb and is a fragment.

FRAGMENT   The new policy to provide coverage on the basis of hours worked.

  READER'S REACTION: I can't tell what the policy *does* or *is*.

EDITED   The new policy **provides** coverage on the basis of hours worked.

• Test #2: Can you turn a word group into a question that can be answered *yes* or *no*? If you can, it's a sentence.

  Caution: Begin your question with *did*. If you begin with *is, are, has,* or *have*, you may provide a missing verb.

WORD GROUPS   They signed the petition to recall the mayor. Suspecting his involvement.

QUESTIONS   Did they sign the petition to recall the mayor? [Yes.] Did suspecting his involvement? [Can't answer.]

CONCLUSION   The first word group is a sentence, but not the second.

Subordinating words.   Look for a **clause** (a word group with a subject and verb) introduced by a subordinating conjunction (*although, if, because, unless;* see 25b) or a pronoun (*that, what, which, who*). If it's not attached to a main clause that can stand alone, it's a fragment.

STRATEGY Hunt for a subordinating word.

FRAGMENT   Residents love the mild climate. Which is ideal for outdoor events.

EDITED   Residents love the mild climate, **which** is ideal for outdoor events.

15a
frag

15b Editing sentence fragments

Complete or attach fragments so that you supply what's missing.

STRATEGY **Attach, rewrite, add, or omit.**

- Attach a fragment to a nearby sentence.

FRAGMENT	Trauma centers give prompt care to heart attack victims. Because **rapid treatment can minimize heart damage.**
ATTACHED	Trauma centers give prompt care to heart attack victims **because** rapid treatment can minimize heart damage.

- Rewrite to eliminate the fragment.

FRAGMENT	**Introducing competing varieties of crabs into the same tank.** He did this in order to study aggression.
REWRITTEN	He **introduced** competing varieties of crabs into the same tank in order to study aggression.

- Drop a subordinating word.

FRAGMENT	Although **the club contested the motion.** It still passed by a majority.
EDITED	The club contested the motion. It still passed by a majority.

- Supply a missing word.

FRAGMENT	**The judge allowing adopted children to meet their natural parents.**
EDITED	The judge **favors** allowing adopted children to meet their natural parents.

15b
frag

15c Using partial sentences

Especially in advertising and creative writing, you'll see *deliberate* fragments used for emphasis or contrast. Use such fragments only when readers will recognize your intention and accept the resulting style. In most academic and professional writing, avoid them.

16 | Comma Splices and Fused Sentences

You may confuse or annoy readers if you inappropriately join two or more sentences using either a comma (**comma splice**) or no punctuation at all (**fused sentence**).

COMMA SPLICE	CBS was founded in 1928 by William S. Paley, his uncle and his father sold him a struggling radio network.
	READER'S REACTION: At first I thought that CBS had three founders: Paley, his uncle, and his father.
EDITED	CBS was founded in 1928 by William S. Paley **;** his uncle and his father sold him a struggling radio network.
FUSED SENTENCE	The city had only one swimming pool without an admission fee the pool was in disrepair.
	READER'S REACTION: Is there only one pool, or only one that's free?
EDITED	The city had only one swimming pool **, but** without an admission fee, the pool was in disrepair.

A **comma splice** links what could be two sentences with a comma alone. A **fused** (or **run-on**) sentence joins what could be two sentences without any punctuation mark or connecting word at all. Either can confuse a reader about where one part ends and another begins.

16
CS

16a Recognizing comma splices

Look for sentences with word groups that could stand on their own but are joined by a comma.

STRATEGY Hunt for commas that string word groups together.

COMMA
SPLICE
The typical Navajo husband is a trustee, the wife and her children own the property.

EDITED
The typical Navajo husband is a trustee **,** **but** the wife and her children own the property.

READER'S REACTION: Until you added *but*, I missed your point about the wife's status.

16b Recognizing fused sentences

Though fused sentences may be any length, look for long sentences with little or no internal punctuation.

STRATEGY Count the statements in a sentence.

If you find several, check the punctuation and connecting words.

FUSED
SENTENCE
The scientists had trouble identifying the fossil it resembled a bird and a lizard.

EDITED
The scientists had trouble identifying the fossil **because** it resembled a bird and a lizard.

READER'S REACTION: Adding *because* separates the two main points and clarifies the sentence.

16c
cs/fs

16c Editing comma splices and fused sentences

As you repair sentences, decide how to relate or connect ideas.

STRATEGY Separate or relate ideas for emphasis.

- Divide into two sentences.
  (_____. _____.)

  FUSED SENTENCE   Football does not cause the most injuries in college gymnastics is more dangerous.

  EDITED   Football does not cause the most injuries in college● **G**ymnastics is more dangerous.

- Join with a comma plus *and, but, or, for, nor, so,* or *yet.*
  (_____, and _____.)

  FUSED SENTENCE   The clinic is understaffed it still performs well.

  EDITED   The clinic is understaffed**❟ yet** it still performs well.

- Connect similar or equal ideas with a semicolon.
  (_____; _____.)

  COMMA SPLICE   An autopilot corrects drift, the system senses and reacts to changes in the aircraft's motion.

  EDITED   An autopilot corrects drift**❟** the system senses and reacts to changes in the aircraft's motion.

- Make one part subordinate to relate ideas.
  (Because _____, _____.)

  A subordinator (*because, though, when, unless*) or relative pronoun (*who, which, that*) can show how one idea depends on another (see 25b).

  COMMA SPLICE   Automobiles are so complex, mechanics may train for years.

  EDITED   **Because** automobiles are so complex**❟** mechanics may train for years.

- Clarify how parts relate with words and a semicolon.
  (_____; therefore, ____.)

  Use words like *however* and *moreover* (conjunctive adverbs, see 25a) or *for example, consequently,* or *in contrast* <u>plus</u> a semicolon.

16c
cs/fs

FUSED SENTENCE	Chickens reach market size within months the lobster takes six to eight years.
EDITED	Chickens reach market size within months $\boldsymbol{;}$ **in contrast** $\boldsymbol{,}$ the lobster takes six to eight years.

ESL ADVICE: Similar Connecting Words

Some connecting words may mean the same thing but need different punctuation. The most common pair is *but* and *however*.

Jose likes his job $\boldsymbol{,}$ **but** the hours are long.

Jose likes his job $\boldsymbol{;}$ **however** $\boldsymbol{,}$ the hours are long.

Because introduces a clause with a subject and verb; *because of* introduces a prepositional phrase.

Because the pay is low, Anna wants a new job.

Because of the low pay, Anna wants a new job.

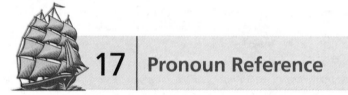

17 | Pronoun Reference

When you replace nouns with pronouns, you reduce repetition as you build connections. If readers can't tell which word is replaced, they may be irritated trying to figure out what your sentence means.

ESL

17 pr ref

AMBIGUOUS REFERENCE	In the circus, Brad's chores included leading the elephants from the cages and hosing **them** down.
	READER'S REACTION: What got hosed down? Elephants? Cages? Both?
EDITED	In the circus, Brad's chores included hosing the elephants down after leading **them** from **their** cages.

Most problems occur when an **antecedent**—the word or words to which
the pronoun refers—isn't clear. By creating clear pronoun reference, you
tie ideas together, clarify relationships, and focus readers' attention.

17a Recognizing unclear pronoun reference

If readers say they "can't figure out what you're saying," make sure that
each pronoun refers clearly to only one possible antecedent that is stated
specifically and located close enough to make the connection clear.

STRATEGY Mark a clear antecedent for each pronoun.

- Can you underline a *single, clear* antecedent?

  AMBIGUOUS REFERENCE
  Robespierre disagreed with Danton over the path the
  French Revolution should take. **He** believed that the
  Revolution was endangered by internal enemies.

  **READER'S REACTION: I'm lost. Who's *he*? Robespierre or
  Danton?**

  EDITED
  Robespierre disagreed with Danton over the path the
  French Revolution should take. **Robespierre** believed that
  the Revolution was endangered by internal enemies.

- Can you answer, "What does [pronoun *X*] refer to?"

  IMPLIED ANTECEDENT
  A hard frost damaged local citrus groves, but **it** has not
  been determined.

  **READER'S REACTION: What does *it* mean—the frost? The
  damage?**

  STATED
  A hard frost damaged local citrus groves, but **the extent of
  the loss** has not been determined.

17b
pr ref

17b Editing pronoun reference

Focus on the pronoun. If needed, clarify the antecedent or rewrite.

STRATEGY Specify or explain the pronoun.

- Replace the pronoun with the noun to which it refers or with a synonym, or reword.

AMBIGUOUS REFERENCE	Detaching the measuring probe from the glass cylinder is a delicate job because **it** breaks easily.
	READER'S REACTION: Which is so fragile, the probe or the cylinder?
REPLACED WITH NOUN	Detaching the measuring probe from the glass cylinder is a delicate job because **the probe** breaks easily.
REWORDED	Because the measuring probe breaks easily, detaching it from the glass cylinder is a delicate job.

- Right after *which*, *this*, or *that*, specify or explain the word to which the pronoun refers.

VAGUE REFERENCE	Redfish have suffered from oil pollution and the destruction of their swamp habitat. **This** has reduced the redfish population.
	READER'S REACTION: Does *this* refer to the destruction of habitat, the pollution, or both?
SPECIFIED	Redfish have suffered from oil pollution and the destruction of their swamp habitat. **This combination** has reduced the redfish population.

Sometimes a pronoun doesn't have to be replaced, just moved—especially to place *who*, *which*, and *that* right after their antecedents.

STRATEGY Move the pronoun close to its antecedent.

CONFUSING	After our dog died, I found an old ball behind **a bush that he loved to chase.**
EDITED	After our dog died, I found behind a bush an **old ball that he loved to chase.**

Especially for many academic readers, a possessive noun used as an antecedent will seem like an error.

STRATEGY **Eliminate the possessive, and rewrite.**

INAPPROPRIATE   In Faulkner's *The Sound and the Fury*, **he** begins from the point of view of a mentally retarded person.

EDITED   In *The Sound and the Fury*, **Faulkner** begins from the point of view of a mentally retarded person.

Remedy problems and guide readers by creating a **reference chain** of pronouns whose antecedent is stated in the first sentence of a passage.

UNCLEAR   Sand paintings were a remarkable form of Pueblo art. An artist would sprinkle dried sand of different colors, ground flower petals, corn pollen, and similar materials onto the floor to create **them.** Encouraging the spirits to send good fortune to humans was **their** purpose.

Because *them* and *their* are buried at the ends of sentences in the middle of the paragraph, readers may lose sight of the topic, sand paintings.

EDITED TO
CREATE A
REFERENCE
CHAIN   Sand paintings were a remarkable form of Pueblo art. To create **them**, artists would sprinkle dried sand of different colors, ground flower petals, corn pollen, and similar materials onto the floor. **Their** purpose was to encourage the spirits to send good fortune to humans.

STRATEGY **Create a reference chain.**

* State the antecedent clearly in the opening sentence.
* Let no other possible antecedents interrupt the chain's links.
* Don't interrupt the chain and try to return to it later.
* Place the pronouns prominently (usually beginning sentences); vary their positions only slightly.

17b
pr ref

18 Agreement

You give readers mixed signals if you don't coordinate sentence parts.

INCONSISTENT   The city council and the mayor is known for her skillful responses to civic debate.

> **READER'S REACTION: This sentence opens with two things—the city council and the mayor—but *is* and *her* seem to switch to only the mayor.**

EDITED   The city council and the mayor **are** known for **their** skillful responses to civic debate.

Readers expect to see how ideas in a sentence relate to each other grammatically—by showing **agreement** in number, person, and gender.

18a Recognizing agreement

A subject and verb in a sentence should agree in number and person. A pronoun (*I, you, she*) should agree with its **antecedent**, the noun or other pronoun to which it refers, in number, person, and gender.

> ### AGREEMENT: NUMBER, PERSON, GENDER
>
> - **Number** shows singular (one) or plural (two or more) items.
>   This **community** needs its recreation center.
>   These **communities** need to share their facilities.
> - **Person** indicates the speaker or subject spoken to or about.
>   FIRST PERSON (SPEAKER)   I, we
>   SECOND PERSON (SPOKEN TO)   You, you
>   THIRD PERSON (SPOKEN ABOUT)   He, she, it, they
> - **Gender** refers to masculine (*he, him*), feminine (*she, her*), or neuter (*it*) qualities attributed to a noun or pronoun.

18b Editing subject-verb agreement

Subjects and verbs should match, both singular or both plural.

STRATEGY **Check the -s and -es endings.**

Add -s or -es to make nouns plural but present tense verbs singular.

SINGULAR   The dam prevent**s** flooding. [third person]

PLURAL   The dam**s** prevent flooding.

Exceptions

- **Nouns with irregular plurals** (*person/people, child/children*) or with the same form for singular and plural (*moose/moose*)
- **Verbs with irregular forms,** including *be* and *have*

More complicated sentences may lead you to use the wrong verb form.

STRATEGY **Find the *real* subject, and match the verb.**

- Mark the subject (not nouns in other word groups). Decide whether it's singular or plural. Edit the verb (or change the subject) to agree.

  DRAFT   The use of new testing **techniques** have increased.

  REAL SUBJECT The <u>use</u> of new testing **techniques** <u>have increased</u>.

  EDITED   The **use** of new testing techniques **has increased**.

- Imagine the core sentence without any intervening expressions. Make the central noun and verb agree.

  DRAFT   A regular tune-up, along with frequent oil changes, pro-
                    long the life of your car.

                    IMAGINE: A regular tune-up, ~~along with frequent oil changes~~, <u>prolong</u> the life of your car.

  EDITED   A regular tune-up, along with frequent oil changes, <u>prolongs</u> the life of your car.

18b
s-v agr

ESL ADVICE: Separated Subjects and Verbs

Check for agreement if the subject and verb are separated.

PHRASE　　　　A person **with sensitive eyes** has to wear sunglasses.

CLAUSE　　　　A person **whose eyes are sensitive** has to wear sunglasses.

When the subject is the same in both clauses, the verbs must agree.

SAME SUBJECT　　A person who wants to protect her eyes wears sunglasses.

Deciding whether some nouns are singular or plural can be tricky.

STRATEGY Use a pronoun to test your verb choice.

Decide which pronoun accurately represents a complicated subject: *he*, *she*, or *it* (singular) or *they* (plural). Read your sentence aloud using this replacement pronoun; edit the verb to agree.

DRAFT　　　　The **news** about the job market [sounds? sound?] good.
　　　　　　　PRONOUN TEST: I could replace "The news" with "it" and say "It sounds."

EDITED　　　　The **news** about the job market **sounds** good.

ESL

18b
s-v agr

TRICKY SINGULAR AND PLURAL NOUNS

- Collective noun identifying a group: *audience, herd, tribe*

    SINGULAR　　The staff is hardworking. [group as a unit = *it*]
    PLURAL　　　The staff are caring people. [individual members = *they*]

- Titles of books or names of companies with plural nouns

    SINGULAR　　*Hard Times* is a great novel.
    SINGULAR　　Burgers to Go is profitable.

- Nouns with plural forms and singular meanings: *politics, mumps*
  SINGULAR   Economics is a popular field of study.
- Compound subjects joined by *and: the men and women*
  PLURAL   Ham and eggs are the main ingredient. [two units]
  SINGULAR   Ham and eggs is my favorite meal. [rarely one unit]
- Alternative subjects joined by *or* (*nor*): *the servers or the cook*
  The verb agrees with the *closer* noun.

  The auditor or the **accountants** review the statement.

  The accountants or the **auditor** reviews the statement.
- Subjects renamed after linking verbs (*is, seems, appears*)
  The verb agrees with the subject (not the words renaming it).

  The chief **obstacle** to change is the mayor and her allies.

Indefinite pronouns do not refer to specific ideas, people, or things. Most (*anyone, each*) require singular verbs, but a few (*both, few*) need plural verbs. Some (*all, most, some*) may take either verb form—singular to refer to something that cannot be counted or plural to refer to two or more items of something that can be counted. (See 222-R.)

SINGULAR   **All** of the food **is** gone.
                  food = food in general (not countable)

PLURAL   **All** of the supplies **are** gone.
                  supplies = many kinds (countable)

ESL ADVICE: Quantifiers

Quantifiers (*each, one, many*) show the amount or quantity of a noun.

EXPRESSIONS FOLLOWED BY PLURAL NOUN + SINGULAR VERB
Each of/Every one of/One of/None of   the **students** lives on
                                             campus.
EXPRESSIONS FOLLOWED BY PLURAL NOUN + PLURAL VERB
Several of/Many of/Both of   the **students** live off campus.

ESL

18b
s-v agr

EXPRESSIONS FOLLOWED BY A SINGULAR OR A PLURAL VERB

                                       noncount noun + singular verb

Some of/Most of/All of/A lot of   the **produce** is fresh.

                                       plural noun + plural verb

Some of/Most of/A lot of/All of   the **vegetables** are fresh.

MUCH **AND** *MOST* **(WITHOUT** *OF***)**

NONCOUNT NOUN   **Much traffic** occurs during rush hour.

PLURAL NOUN   **Most Americans** live in or near cities.

TRICKY SINGULAR AND PLURAL PRONOUNS

- *Who, which,* and *that* as subjects of clauses

  Match the verb and the word to which the pronoun refers.

  > He likes a film that builds suspense but novels that show character.

- *Each* or *every* before a compound subject

  SINGULAR   Each clerk and manager checks the log.

- *Each* and *every* after a compound subject

  PLURAL   The clerks and managers each check the log.

18c   Editing pronoun-antecedent agreement

Work with either the pronoun or its **antecedent,** the word to which it refers. Edit to bring the other into agreement.

STRATEGY   Mark the specific word to which a pronoun refers.

INCONSISTENT   **Each** of the samples travels in their own case.

CLEAR   **Each** of the samples travels in its own case.

When **indefinite pronouns** (see 222-R) are singular, so are other pronouns that refer to them.

Somebody on the team left her racket on the court.

Each of the men has his own equipment.

To avoid sexist language, use plural pronouns and antecedents.

SEXIST	**Everybody** used charts in **his** sales **talk.**
INFORMAL (SPOKEN)	**Everybody** used charts in **their** sales **talks.**
WRITTEN	**All presenters** used charts in **their** sales **talks.**

ESL ADVICE: *This, That, These, Those*

To modify nouns, *this* and *that* are singular; *these* and *those* are plural.

INCONSISTENT	This crystals make snowflakes.
PLURAL	**These crystals** make snowflakes.
INCONSISTENT	Those experiment takes two days.
SINGULAR	**That experiment** takes two days.

19 | Correct Forms

ESL

19 verb

If you misuse word forms, readers may doubt your ability as a writer and pay more attention to the error than to your point.

DRAFT	By Friday, him and me will submit the report.
	READER'S REACTION: *Him and me* sounds uneducated. Who hired this person?
EDITED	By Friday, **he and I** will submit the report.

Most readers expect you to edit your writing to use widely accepted forms of verbs, pronouns, adjectives, and adverbs.

19a Recognizing and editing verb forms

Verbs vary in **tense** as they show past, present, and future time.

Past tense -*ed* ending for regular verbs. Be sure to write this ending even if you don't hear it pronounced before a -*d* or -*t* sound.

DRAFT	The company **use** to provide dental benefits.
EDITED	The company **used** to provide dental benefits.

Past tense irregular verbs. Irregular verbs form the past tense in some way other than adding -*ed* (*run/ran*). (For a list, see p. 218-R.)

DRAFT	The movie characters **sweared** constantly.
EDITED	The movie characters **swore** constantly.

Verb forms in complex tenses. Complex tenses (see p. 213-R) have a main verb and a helping verb (see p. 215-R). The main verb is a **participle, past** (-*ed*, -*en*, or irregular form) or **present** (-*ing* form). The helping verb is a form of *be, do,* or *have* or a verb such as *will* or *would*.

	helping verb + main verb (present participle)
-ING FORM	He was **loading** the delivery van.
	helping verb + main verb (past participle)
REGULAR VERB	Mike has **analyzed** the problem.
IRREGULAR VERB	Lynn has **brought** the equipment.

19a
verb

Helping verbs in progressive tenses. These past, present, and future forms show an action in progress using an -*ing* main verb: *is turning, was turning, will be turning.* (See the chart on p. 214-R.) In writing, use all the parts of the correct verb even if your spoken dialect omits them.

WORD OMITTED	The interview **starting** now.
EDITED	The interview **is starting** now.
WRONG FORM	The workers **was running** for the door.
EDITED	The workers **were running** for the door.

Past participles in perfect tenses. The present, past, and future perfect tenses combine a helping verb with the past participle (the *-ed, -en,* or irregular form) to show the order of events. (See the chart on p. 214-R.) Don't substitute the simple past tense for the past participle.

MISTAKEN PAST	Pete **had rode** for a year before his injury.
EDITED	Pete **had ridden** for a year before his injury.

Subjunctive mood. Sentences can be classified by mood, the form of the verb that reflects the writer's or speaker's attitude.

- **Indicative:** statements intended as truthful or factual

  Motorcycle helmets **have reduced** injuries.

- **Imperative:** statements acting as commands

  Get a helmet.

- **Subjunctive:** statements expressing uncertainty—a supposition, prediction, possibility, desire, or wish

  If you **were** to crash, the helmet would protect your head.

  Jim's insurance requires that he **wear** a helmet.

The subjunctive appears in formal writing, often in **conditional statements** beginning with *if* (for examples, see p. 216-R) and in *that* clauses with verbs such as *ask* or *request.* With *that,* use the basic present form (*wear, be*), even with the third person singular. With *if,* use the basic present, the past (*wore, were* not *was*), or the past perfect (*had worn* not *would have worn, had been*).

19a
verb

Lie, lay, sit, set. These forms are confusing for many writers.

VERB	PRESENT	PAST	PAST PARTICIPLE
lie (oneself)	lie	lay	lain
lay (an object)	lay	laid	laid
sit (oneself)	sit	sat	sat
set (an object)	set	set	set

DRAFT	I **laid** down yesterday for a nap. I **have laid** down every afternoon for a week.
EDITED	I **lay** down yesterday for a nap. I **have lain** down every afternoon for a week.
DRAFT	Erica and Steve **sat** the projector on the table.
EDITED	Erica and Steve **set** the projector on the table.

19b Editing for clear tense sequence

Readers expect you to use one tense or to follow a logical sequence.

STRATEGY Change tense to relate events in time.

LOGICAL	People **forget** that four candidates **ran** in 1948.
LOGICAL	The accountant **destroyed** the file because **no one had asked** him to save it.
LOGICAL	No one **had recognized** that food from cans sealed with lead solder **is** poisonous.

19c Recognizing pronoun forms

19c
pron

Pronouns change form to fit their roles in a sentence (see p. 221-R).

SUBJECT   I, you, he, she, it; we, you, they

I ran out of leaflets, but **he** had plenty.

OBJECT	me, you, him, her, it; us, you, them
	Jamie gave **me** some extras for **them.**
POSSESSIVE	my, mine, your, yours, his, her, hers, its; our, ours, your, yours, their, theirs
	Our client chose **my** leaflet design, not **hers.**

Subject complement. A pronoun that renames the subject (a **subject complement**) follows *be* (*is, are, was, were*), using the subjective form.

   subject   subject complement
The people assigned the report <u>were</u> **Trinh and I.**

STRATEGY Test for pronouns that rename the subject.

Reverse the sentence to make the pronoun the subject.

DRAFT	**The last art majors** to get jobs were Becky and **me.**
REVERSED	Becky and **me** were the last art majors to get jobs.
REVERSE TEST	**Me** was the last art major. [doesn't fit]
EDITED	The last art majors to get jobs were Becky and **I.**

Possessive pronouns. You may be tempted to add an *'s* to a possessive pronoun just as you do with a noun (**John's** car, the **cat's meow**).

STRATEGY Test your possessive pronouns.

Spell out *it's* as the expression it stands for: *it* + *is*. If the expansion fits, keep the apostrophe. If not, omit it.

DRAFT	The food pantry gave away all **it's** tuna.
TEST	The food pantry gave away all **it is** tuna.
EDITED	The food pantry gave away all **its** tuna.

19c
pron

19d Editing pronoun forms

Compound subjects and objects. Use the same form for a pronoun in a compound that you would use if it were by itself.

STRATEGY **Try focus-imagine-choose.**

- **Focus** on the questionable pronoun.

    DRAFT   Anna and **me** will develop the video.
                   FOCUS: *I* or *me?*

- **Imagine** each choice for the pronoun.

    Me will develop the video. (no)

    I will develop the video. (yes)

- **Choose** the correct form for the compound.

    EDITED   Anna and **I** will develop the video.

Appositives. When you rename a preceding noun or pronoun in an **appositive**, match the pronoun to the form of the word being renamed.

STRATEGY **Test possible replacements.**

DRAFT	The two illustrators on the panel, **her** and **me,** answered questions.
REPLACEMENT	**Her** and **me** answered questions. (no)
REPLACEMENT	**She** and **I** answered questions. (yes)
EDITED	The two illustrators on the panel, **she and I,** answered questions.

Comparisons with *than* or *as.* When you end a comparison with a pronoun, choose the form based on the information left out.

SUBJECT	I gave her sister more help than **she** [did].
OBJECT	I gave her sister more help than [I gave] **her.**

***Who* and *whom*.** Choose *who* and *whoever* as subjects; choose *whom* and *whomever* as objects. When the pronoun is in a clause, make your choice based on its role within the clause, not the sentence as a whole.

SUBJECT	The boy **who wins the race** will get the prize.
SUBJECT	The fine must be paid by **whoever holds the deed.**
SUBJECT	**Who** has a reader's sympathy, Huck or Jim?
OBJECT	Give this task to **whomever you trust.**
OBJECT	**Whom** can Cordelia trust as the scene ends?

19e Recognizing adjectives and adverbs

Adjectives and adverbs **modify** other words, adding to, qualifying, limiting, or extending their meaning.

FEATURES OF ADJECTIVES AND ADVERBS

ADJECTIVES

- Modify nouns and pronouns
- Answer "How many?" "What kind?" "Which one (or ones)?" "What size, color, or shape?"
- Include words like *blue, complicated,* and *good*
- Include words created by adding endings like *-able, -ical, -less, -ful,* and *-ous* to nouns or verbs (*sociological, nervous, seamless*)

ADVERBS

- Modify verbs, adjectives, and other adverbs
- Modify phrases (*almost* over the hill), clauses (*soon after* I added the eggs), and sentences (*Remarkably,* the mechanism was unharmed).
- Answer "When?" "Where?" "How?" "How often?" "Which direction?" "What degree?"
- Include mostly words ending in *-ly* (*quickly*) but also some words that do not end in *-ly* (*fast, very, well, quite, late*)

19e
adj/adv

19f   Editing adjectives and adverbs

Because not all adverbs end in -*ly* and some adjectives do (*friendly*), the
-*ly* ending won't always help you pick the right form. If you can't tell
which to use, ask the questions in the chart on p. 143.

DRAFT   Write **careful** so the directions are clear.

> QUESTION: Write *how*? It answers an adverb question.

EDITED   Write **carefully** so the directions are clear.

STRATEGY Draw an arrow.

Point to the word that is modified. If it acts as a noun or pronoun, select
an adjective; if it acts as a verb, adjective, or adverb, use an adverb.

DRAFT   The insulation underwent **remarkable** quick deteriora-
                  tion.

> CONNECTION: *Remarkable* modifies *quick* (and answers the
> adverb question "How quick?"). (*Quick* in turn modifies
> *deterioration* and answers the adjective question "What
> kind of deterioration?") Replace *remarkable* with an ad-
> verb.

EDITED   The insulation underwent **remarkably** quick deterioration.

Modifiers with linking verbs. Verbs such as *look*, *feel*, and *prove* can
show both states of being (**linking verbs**) and activities (**action verbs**).
Use an adjective for a state of being and an adverb for an activity.

ADJECTIVE (BEING) The metal cover over the motor turned **hot.**

ADVERB (ACTION)   The large wheel turned **quickly.**

ADJECTIVE   The movement grew **rapid.** [The motion became quick.]

ADVERB   The movement grew **rapidly.** [The group spread its ideas.]

Real/really, bad/badly, good/well, sure/surely. Informal uses of
these words may be accepted in speech but not in formal writing.

INFORMAL   I feel **badly** that our group argues so much.

READER'S REACTION: **Someone who *feels badly* has a poor sense of touch.**

TRICKY ADJECTIVES AND ADVERBS

BAD/BADLY

Use *bad* (adjective) with linking verbs (*is, seems, appears*).
Use *badly* (adverb) with action verbs.

I feel **bad** that our group argues so much.
The new breathing apparatus works **badly.**

GOOD/WELL

Use *good* (adjective) with linking verbs (*is, seems*)
Use *well* (adverb) with action verbs unless it refers to health.

The chef's new garlic dressing tastes **good.**
The new pump works **well.**
Nan looks **well.** [health]

REAL/REALLY

Use *really* (adverb), not *real,* to modify an adjective or adverb.

Lu Ming is **really** efficient.
Lu Ming works **really** efficiently.

SURE/SURELY

Use *surely* (adverb) to modify an adjective.

This map is **surely** misleading.

Double negatives. Readers are likely to feel that two negatives (*no, none, not, never, hardly, scarcely, don't*) cancel each other out.

DRAFT   The nurses **can't hardly** manage the emergencies.

READER'S REACTION: **This sounds more like a conversation than a report.**

EDITED   The nurses **can hardly** manage the emergencies.

19g Recognizing and editing comparisons

For most modifiers, choose the form based on how many things you compare: **positive** (no others), **comparative** (two things; *-er* or *more*), **superlative** (three or more things; *-est* or *most*). (See p. 223-R.)

19g
adj/adv

POSITIVE	The liquid flowed **quickly** into the **large** beaker.
COMPARATIVE	The liquid flowed **more quickly** into the **larger** beaker.
SUPERLATIVE	The liquid flowed **most quickly** into the **largest** beaker.

STRATEGY Use precise comparative forms.

INACCURATE	Of the four age groups (20–29, 30–44, 45–59, and 60+), those in the older group smoked least.
	READER'S REACTION: Did those in the older *groups* or the *oldest group* smoke least?
PRECISE	Of the four age groups (20–29, 30–44, 45–59, and 60+), those in the **oldest group** smoked least.

Most readers won't accept double comparative forms.

DRAFT	Jorge is the **most agilest** athlete.
EDITED	Jorge is the **most agile** athlete.

Illogical comparisons. Some adjectives and adverbs, such as *unique, impossible, pregnant,* and *dead,* can't logically take comparative forms.

ILLOGICAL	Gottlieb's "Nightscape" is **most unique.**
	READER'S REACTION: How can this painting be *more* or *most* if it's *unique*—the only one?
LOGICAL	Gottlieb's "Nightscape" is **unique.**

19g
adj/adv

SECTION 5
Writing Clearly

Voices from the Community

❝ Plain English means creating a document that is visually inviting, logically organized, and understandable on the first reading. ❞

Nancy M. Smith and Ann D. Wallace, "Plain English at a Glance"

20 | Clear Sentences

Most readers find murky sentences hard to read.

INDIRECT OR EVASIVE	It is suggested that employee work cooperation encouragement be used for product quality improvement. **READER'S REACTION: Who is suggesting this? What is "employee work cooperation encouragement"?**
CLEAR	We will try to improve our products by encouraging employees to work cooperatively.

All communities value clear writing that's easy to read even if it presents complex ideas and reasoning. You can improve foggy sentences by creating clear subjects and verbs and using direct sentence structures.

20a Recognizing unclear sentences

Clear sentences answer the question "Who does what (to whom)?" When a sentence doesn't readily answer this question, try to make its subject and verb easy for readers to identify.

UNCLEAR	One suggestion offered by physicians is that there is a need to be especially observant of a baby's behavior in order to notice any evidence of seizures. **READER'S REACTION: Who's doing the observing?**
CLEAR	Physicians suggest that parents watch babies carefully for evidence of seizures.

20b Editing for clear sentences

Readers need to identify subjects (who) and verbs (did what) easily.

STRATEGY Find your significant subject.

- Ask "Who (or what) am I talking about here?"
- Ask "Is this what I want to emphasize?"

UNFOCUSED	You run the greatest risk if you expose yourself to tanning machines as well as the sun because both can damage the skin.
	READER'S REACTION: Isn't the point the danger posed by sunbathing and tanning? Why are they both buried in the middle?
EDITED	Either **the sun or a tanning machine** can damage the skin, and you run the greatest risk from exposure to **both** of them.

Weak nouns. When you create a noun (*completion, happiness*) from another kind of word such as a verb (*complete*) or an adjective (*happy*), you **nominalize** that word. Replace each weak nominalization with a clear and significant subject (or object). Name the action (did what?) in the verb. Avoid weak, lifeless verbs, especially forms of *be*.

In a **noun string,** one noun modifies another or nouns plus adjectives modify other nouns: *jet lag, computer network server.* Turn the key word in a string (usually the last noun) into a verb or a single noun. Then turn other nouns from the string into prepositional phrases.

CONFUSING	The team did a ceramic valve lining design flaw analysis.
EDITED	The team **analyzed** flaws **in** the lining design **for** ceramic valves.

Weak verbs. Forms of the verb *be* (*is, are, was, were*) show being, not action, and may create dull sentences.

STRATEGY Energize your verbs.

- Use more forceful verbs in place of forms of *be*.

WEAK	The program **is a money saver.**
STRONGER	The program **saves money.**

- Turn nouns into verbs to replace general verbs (*do, give, have, get, provide, shape, make*).

WEAK	We **have done** a <u>study</u> of the project and **will provide** <u>funding</u> for it.
STRONGER	We **have studied** the project and **will fund** it.

- Drop indirect "there is," "there are," and "it is" patterns.

DRAFT	**There is** a need for more classrooms at Kenny School.
EDITED	Kenny School needs more classrooms.

ESL ADVICE: *There* and *It* as Subjects

There and *it* as subjects may not refer to a thing or place (as in *The car is there* or *What did it* [the book, for example] *say?*). *There* may introduce new material, and *it* may refer to weather, time, or distance.

DRAFT	Although there was snowing, it was dancing after dinner.
EDITED	Although **it** was snowing, **there** was dancing after dinner.

Unnecessary passive voice. When you turn the doer or actor of a sentence into the receiver of action, you use the **passive voice** instead of the **active.** (See p. 216-R.) The passive voice focuses on the action, not the agent; the active voice puts the doer into the first, or subject, position.

STRATEGY Reconsider wordy or evasive passive structures.

PASSIVE	**The people** affected by the toxin were contacted by **the Centers for Disease Control.**
ACTIVE	**The Centers for Disease Control** contacted the people affected by the toxin.

Separated subject and verb. Too much distance between a subject and verb can make a sentence difficult to read.

STRATEGY Keep the verb close to the subject.

CONFUSING   The veterinary association, **in response to the costly guidelines for disposal of medical waste,** has created a low-cost loan program for its members.

EDITED   The veterinary association has created a low-cost loan program for its members **in response to the costly guidelines for disposal of medical waste.**

21 | Mixed Structures

When you're reading, you can't ask the writer to explain a confusing shift of topic or a jumbled sentence.

TOPIC SHIFT   One **skill** I envy is **a person** who can meet deadlines.
              READER'S REACTION: Does this mean a *skill* is a *person*?

EDITED   One **skill** I envy is **the ability** to meet deadlines.

Mixed sentences shift topics or grammatical structures unexpectedly, throwing the reader off the track. **Incomplete sentences** lack either grammatical (see 15a) or logical completeness. For example, if an advertiser says that *X* "is better," you expect to hear "than *Y*."

21a Recognizing mixed and incomplete sentences

In most sentences, the subject announces a topic, and the **predicate** (the verb and the words that complete it) comments on or renames the topic. With a **topic shift** (**faulty predication**), the second part of the sentence comments on or names a topic different from the one first announced. With a **mixed grammatical pattern,** the sentence shifts from one pattern to another.

STRATEGY Look for topic and comment.

- Read your sentences aloud for *meaning*, especially how the topic (subject) and comment (predicate) relate.
- Ask "Who does what?" or "What is it?" If the answer is illogical, edit.
- Ask, "What's the topic? How does the rest of the sentence comment on it or rename it?"
- Ask, "Does the sentence clearly tell who does what to whom?"

TOPIC SHIFT   In this factory, **flaws** in the product noticed by any worker **can stop** the assembly line.

        READER'S REACTION: Who does what? Flaws can't stop the line.

EDITED   In this factory, **any worker** who notices flaws in the product **can stop** the assembly line.

21b Editing mixed and incomplete sentences

State your topic; then imagine what readers will expect next.

STRATEGY Rename the subject.

- Keep the topics on each side of *be* equivalent; make sure the second part of the sentence renames the topic in the first part.

TOPIC SHIFT   **Irradiation** is **food** that is preserved by radiation.

EDITED   **Irradiation** is a **process** used to preserve food.

- Drop *is when* and *is where*; they create an imbalance on both sides of *be*.

NOT BALANCED   **Blocking** is **when** a network schedules a less popular program between two popular ones.

EDITED   **Blocking** is the **practice** of scheduling a less popular program between two popular ones.

• Rewrite to eliminate *the reason . . . is because*.

Readers expect the subject (topic) to be renamed after *is*. When *because* appears there instead, they find the sentence illogical.

DRAFT	The **reason** he took up skating **is because** he wanted winter exercise.
EDITED	The reason he took up skating **is that** he wanted winter exercise. [Change *because* to *that*.]
EDITED	He took up skating **because** he wanted winter exercise. [Drop *the reason . . . is*.]

Inconsistent sentence patterns. If you mistake words between the subject and verb for the sentence topic, you may mix up different patterns.

> STRATEGY **Make the topic for subject and verb the same.**

TOPIC SHIFT	Programming **decisions** by TV executives <u>consider</u> the need for audience share.
	READER'S REACTION: How can decisions think?
EDITED	When **making** programming decisions, **TV executives** <u>consider</u> the need for audience share.

Incomplete and illogical comparisons. You can sometimes simplify by omitting repeated elements that readers can supply. But if you cut essentials, you may create an **incomplete comparison,** missing words needed for clarity, or an **illogical comparison,** comparing things that aren't comparable.

> STRATEGY **Add missing words or a possessive to compare logically.**

ILLOGICAL	The fat content in even a small hamburger is more than a skinless chicken breast.
	READER'S REACTION: The fat is more than the chicken breast?
EDITED	The fat content in even a small hamburger is more than **that in** a skinless chicken breast.

EDITED   Even a small **hamburger's** fat content is more than a skinless chicken **breast's.**

22 | Dangling and Misplaced Modifiers

Readers generally expect to find related parts of a sentence together.

MISPLACED
MODIFIER   The wife believes she sees a living figure behind the wallpaper in the story by Charlotte Perkins Gilman, which adds to her sense of entrapment.
READER'S REACTION: How could a story add to a feeling of entrapment?

MODIFIER MOVED   The wife **in the story by Charlotte Perkins Gilman** believes she sees a living figure behind the wallpaper, which adds to her sense of entrapment.

Because a **modifier** qualifies, adds to, or limits the meaning of another word or word group, it needs to be positioned logically. Otherwise, readers may find a sentence vague, illogical, or even humorous.

22a Recognizing misplaced modifiers

To recognize a **misplaced modifier,** look for a word or word group that is not positioned closely enough to the word or words it modifies—its **headword**—and instead appears to modify some other word.

MISPLACED   The caterer served food to the clients standing around the room on flimsy paper plates.
READER'S REACTION: Surely the clients weren't standing on the plates!

MOVED   The caterer served food **on flimsy paper plates** to the clients standing around the room.

Dangling modifier. To spot a **dangling modifier,** look for a sentence that begins with a modifier but doesn't name the person, idea, or thing modified. Readers will think the modifier refers to the subject of the sentence that follows. If it doesn't, the modifier dangles.

DANGLING   **Looking** for a way to reduce complaints from non-smokers, **a ventilation fan** was installed.
                     READER'S REACTION: How could a fan look for anything?

SUBJECT ADDED   **Looking** for a way to reduce complaints from nonsmokers, **the company** installed a ventilation fan.

Squinting modifier. To recognize a **squinting modifier,** look for a word that appears to modify both the word before and the word after. Squinting modifiers are often misplaced **limiting modifiers,** words like *only, almost, hardly, just, scarcely,* and *even.* Limiting modifiers can move around in a sentence, generally changing meaning as they do.

SQUINTING   People who abuse alcohol **often** have other problems.
                     READER'S REACTION: Do they *drink often* or *often have* other problems?

EDITED   People who **often** abuse alcohol tend to have other problems.

Split infinitives. Some readers find words placed between the parts of an infinitive (*to* plus a verb) irritating. Balance this risk against the directness a split infinitive sometimes offers.

IRRITATING?   The dancers moved **to very rapidly align** themselves.
EDITED   The dancers moved **very rapidly to align** themselves.

22b Editing misplaced modifiers

Make sure modifiers clearly relate to the words they qualify.

STRATEGY Position and connect modifiers logically.

- Place *who*, *which*, or *that* close to its headword.

  MISPLACED   The inspectors discovered another tank behind the building that was leaking toxic waste.

  MOVED   **Behind the building,** the inspectors discovered another tank that was leaking toxic waste.

- State the word being modified.

  DANGLING   While shopping, a stuffed alligator caught my eye.

  SUBJECT ADDED While **I was** shopping, a stuffed alligator caught my eye.

- Ask, "What do I really mean here? Who's doing what?" Then rework the sentence to state that point as directly as possible.

  DANGLING   After debating changes in the regulations for months, the present standards were allowed to continue.
  READER'S REACTION: *Who* is debating? Not the standards!

  REWRITTEN   The commission debated changes in the regulations for months but decided to continue the present standards.

23 | Unnecessary Shifts

Especially in formal contexts, readers expect logically consistent writing.

SHIFTED   If **parents** called the school board, **we** could explain why **we** oppose the new policy.
    READER'S REACTION: I'm confused. Who should do what?

EDITED   If **parents** called the school board, **they** could explain why **they** oppose the new policy.

Although listeners tolerate shifts during conversation—or ask for clarification—readers are likely to be irritated by illogical shifts.

23a Recognizing shifts in person and number

A shift in **person** occurs when you switch illogically from one perspective (*I, you, he,* or *she*) to another. A shift in **number** occurs when you illogically switch sentence elements, especially pronouns and **antecedents** (the words to which they refer), between singular and plural.

INCONSISTENT   When **a business executive** is looking for a new job, **they** often consult a placement service.
                READER'S REACTION: Who is "they"? The executive?

EDITED   When **business executives are** looking for **new jobs, they** often consult a placement service.

FIRST, SECOND, AND THIRD PERSON IN THREE COMMUNITIES

- **First person singular (*I*).** Use *I* to refer to yourself as the writer or person whose experiences and perceptions are an essay's subject. Readers may find *I* too personal in some formal academic contexts, especially in the sciences.
- **First person plural (*we*).** Use *we* in a collaborative project with several authors. In some academic papers, you may use *we* as you refer to ideas you and your readers share. *We* is common at work and in public when you represent or appeal to your organization.
- **Second person (*you*).** Use *you* to refer directly to the reader ("you, the reader"). In most academic and work writing, readers find *you* inappropriate, but some situations call for *you*, as in a set of instructions or a plain-language contract. In public writing that urges action, *you* can engage the reader in a civic appeal.
- **Third person (*he, she, it, they, one, someone,* and comparable pronouns).** Use these pronouns to refer to the ideas, things, and people you write about, including *people, person,* and names of groups (such as *students*). Avoid sexist use of *he* and *she.* Be alert to exclusionary uses of pronouns, such as inappropriately pitting *we* against *they.*

23b Editing shifts in person and number

Reflect a consistent perspective in person and number.

STRATEGY **Match references, and edit for consistency.**

- Do nouns and pronouns refer to the same person?
- Are they consistently singular or plural?

SINGULAR   If **a person** has some money to invest, **he or she** should seek financial advice.

PLURAL   If **people** have some money to invest, **they** should seek financial advice.

23c Recognizing shifts in tense

The **tense** of a verb indicates time as past, present, or future (see 213-R). When you change tense within a passage, you signal a change in time and the relationship of events. Illogical shifts can mislead your readers.

ILLOGICAL SHIFT   Scientists **discovered** nests that **indicated** how some dinosaurs **take care** of their young.

LOGICAL   Scientists **discovered** nests that **indicate** how some dinosaurs **took care** of their young.

ESL ADVICE: Verb Tense and Expressions of Time

Use both verb tense and time expressions (*today, soon*) to show changes in time. Keep these consistent.

INCONSISTENT   I **study** English last year, and now I **worked** for an American company.

EDITED   I **studied** English last year, and now I **work** for an American company.

23d Editing shifts in tense

Shift tense because your account or convention requires the change.

STRATEGY **Match your verbs to your intended time.**

INCONSISTENT SHIFT TO PRESENT	We **had been searching** for a festival site when suddenly Tonia **yells,** "This is it!"
EDITED	We **had been searching** for a festival site when suddenly Tonia **yelled,** "This is it!"

Follow convention, and use present tense when you summarize or analyze events or information from a work such as a novel or film.

INCONSISTENT	As the novel begins, Ishmael **comes** to New Bedford to ship out on a whaler, which he soon **did.**
CONVENTIONAL	As the novel begins, Ishmael **comes** to New Bedford to ship out on a whaler, which he soon **does.**

24 | Parallelism

When you use consistent patterns, readers can follow your ideas easily and concentrate on your meaning because they know what to expect.

WEAK	Hal furnished his apartment with what he purchased at flea markets, buying items from want ads, and gifts from friends. **READER'S REACTION: This list seems wordy and jumbled.**
PARALLEL	Hal furnished his apartment with **purchases from flea markets,** **items from want ads,** and **gifts from friends**.

Parallelism is the expression of similar or related ideas in similar grammatical form; it creates sentence rhythms and highlights ideas.

24a Recognizing faulty parallelism

Once you begin a parallel pattern, you need to complete it.

MIXED   Swimming is an exercise that **aids** cardiovascular fitness, **develops** overall muscle strength, and **probably without causing** injuries.

PARALLEL   Swimming is an exercise that **aids** cardiovascular fitness, **develops** overall muscle strength, and **causes** few injuries.

24b Editing for parallelism

When you place items in a series, pair, or list, make sure they have the same structure even if they differ in length and wording. With the seven coordinating conjunctions (*and, but, or, for, nor, so,* and *yet*), use parallelism to heighten similarities or contrasts.

MIXED   A well-trained scientist keeps a detailed lab notebook and the entries made accurately.

PARALLEL   A well-trained scientist keeps a **detailed and accurate** lab notebook.

Edit each series with the full sentence in mind. If the lead-in word can be the same, don't repeat it. If the lead-in words differ, include them.

INCOMPLETE   The main character in the novel *Tarzan of the Apes* has appeared on television, films, and comic books.
               READER'S REACTION: I doubt he appeared *on* films and *on* comic books.

EDITED   The main character in the novel *Tarzan of the Apes* has appeared **on** television, **in** films, and **in** comic books.

STRATEGY Use parallelism to organize meaning.

• Build up to a key point placed last in a series.

  To complete their campaigns, candidates need stamina, courage, and, most of all, **ambition.**

- List items in parallel form.

  These trends characterized the early 1960s:

    1. **A growing** civil rights movement
    2. **A developing** anticommunist foreign policy
    3. **An increasing** emphasis on youth in culture and politics

- Emphasize clusters of sentences and paragraphs.

  Each of us probably belongs to groups whose values conflict. **You may belong to** a religious organization that **endorses restraint in** alcohol use while **you also belong to** a social group that **accepts drinking. You may belong to** a sports team **that supports** competing and a club **that promotes** cooperation.

- Connect sections of an essay or a report.

  The opening for each paragraph can be a simple parallel element.

  One reason for approving this proposal now is . . .

  A second reason for acting is . . .

  The third, and most important, reason for taking steps is . . .

---

25 | Coordination and Subordination

Suppose you were editing a report with this passage.

California's farmers ship fresh lettuce, avocados, and other produce to supermarkets. They never send fresh olives.

READER'S REACTION: These sentences sound choppy. How do they connect?

Using **coordination,** you could give equal emphasis to the statements.

California's farmers ship fresh lettuce, avocados, and other produce to supermarkets **,** **but** they never send fresh olives.

Using **subordination**, you could show the relative weight of ideas.

California's farmers ship fresh lettuce, avocados, and other produce to supermarkets, **though** they never send fresh olives.

25a Recognizing coordination

Use coordination to link words, phrases, or clauses to emphasize their equal weight, balance the structure, or express addition or opposition.

CREATING AND PUNCTUATING COORDINATION

* Use *and, but, or, for, nor, so,* or *yet* (coordinating conjunctions). Precede them with a comma when joining two main clauses, word groups that could stand on their own as sentences (see p. 210-R).

  cut **and** hemmed   intrigued **yet** suspicious

  The new zoning board met **,** **but** it did not vote.

* Use pairs like *either/or, neither/nor,* and *not only/but also.*

  either music therapy **or** pet therapy

* Use a semicolon.

  Some customers fidgeted **;** others stared at the ceiling.

* Use conjunctive adverbs like *however, moreover, nonetheless, thus,* and *consequently* preceded by a semicolon.

  The managers could speed up the checkout lines **;** **however** **,** they seldom pay much attention to the problem.

* Use a colon.

  Magazine racks by the checkout counters serve a useful purpose **:** they give customers something to read while waiting.

EXPRESSING RELATIONSHIPS THROUGH COORDINATION

RELATIONSHIP	COORDINATING CONJUNCTION	CONJUNCTIVE ADVERB
addition	, and	; in addition, ; furthermore,
opposition or contrast	, but , yet	; in contrast, ; however, ; nonetheless,
result	, so	; therefore, ; consequently, ; thus,
cause	, for	
choice	, or	; otherwise
negation	, nor	

25b Recognizing subordination

Subordination creates sentences with unequal elements: the **main clause** (which could stand alone as a sentence) presents the central idea; at least one **subordinate clause** (which could not stand alone) modifies or comments on it. You signal this unequal relationship by beginning the subordinate clause with a **subordinator** or **relative pronoun,** a word like *while, although,* or *which,* and attaching it to the main clause.

CREATING AND PUNCTUATING SUBORDINATION

- **Use a subordinating conjunction** such as *although* or *because* to create a subordinate clause at the beginning or end of a sentence.

  At the beginning of a sentence: Add a comma *after* an introductory clause that begins with a subordinating conjunction.

  Once she understood the problem, she had no trouble solving it.

At the end of a sentence: Do not use a comma if the clause is *essential* to the meaning of the main clause (restrictive); use a comma if the clause is *not essential* (nonrestrictive). (See 28d.)

ESSENTIAL Radar tracking of flights began **because several airliners collided in midair.**

NONESSENTIAL The present air traffic control system works reasonably well **, although accidents still occur.**

- **Use a relative pronoun** (*who, which, that*) to create a relative clause at the end or in the middle of a sentence. A clause containing information *essential* to the meaning of the main clause begins with *that* and should not be set off with commas. Set off nonessential information. (See 28d.)

ESSENTIAL
(NO COMMA) The anthropologists discovered the site of a building **that early settlers used as a meetinghouse.**

NONESSENTIAL
(COMMA) At one end of the site they found remains of a smaller building **, which may have been a storage shed.**

EXPRESSING RELATIONSHIPS THROUGH SUBORDINATION

RELATIONSHIP	CONJUNCTION OR OTHER WORD
Time	before, while, until, since, once, whenever, whereupon, after, when
Cause	because, since
Result	in order that, so that, so, that
Concession or contrast	although, though, even though, as if, while
Place	where, wherever
Condition	if, whether, provided, unless, rather than
Comparison	as
Identification	that, which, who

25c Editing for coordination and subordination

How can you tell how much coordination or subordination to use? Read your writing aloud. Watch for short, choppy sentences or long, dense passages. Consider your community: academic readers may accept more subordination than work colleagues who favor conciseness.

STRATEGY Replace *and, so,* and *but* to vary or specify.

DRAFT
The fresh grapefruit in supermarkets is picked before it matures to avoid spoilage, **and** it can taste bitter, **but** the grapefruit in cans is picked later, **and** it tastes sweeter.

EDITED
The fresh grapefruit in supermarkets is picked before it matures **,** **so** it can taste bitter. The grapefruit in cans is picked later **;** **consequently**, it tastes sweeter.

Help readers see what matters most; put key ideas in a main clause and secondary ideas in a subordinate clause.

STRATEGY Move a main point to a main clause.

DRAFT
His equipment was inferior, although Jim still set a school record throwing the discus.

READER'S REACTION: Isn't Jim's achievement the point?

EDITED
Although his equipment was inferior, Jim still set a school record throwing the discus.

ESL ADVICE: Structures for Coordination and Subordination

Use both coordinators and subordinators, but don't mix the two.

MIXED
Although frogs can live both on land and in water, **but** they need to breathe oxygen.

CONSISTENT
COORDINATION

Frogs can live on land and in water, **but** they need to breathe oxygen.

CONSISTENT
SUBORDINATION

Although frogs can live on land and in water, they need to breathe oxygen.

26 | Conciseness

When you leave extra words in your writing, you waste the time of readers who value clarity, efficiency, or convincing advocacy.

WORDY   **There is evidence that the use of** pay **as an** incentive **can be a factor** in improvement **of the** quality **of** work.
                READER'S REACTION: Why is this so long-winded?

ABRUPT   Incentive pay improves work quality.

RESHAPED   Incentive pay **often encourages** work **of higher** quality.

Conciseness means using only the words you need—not the fewest possible, but only those that suit your purpose, meaning, and readers.

26a Recognizing common types of wordiness

Look carefully for both unnecessary and repetitive words.

Wordy phrases. Shrink wordy phrases to one or two words—or none.

COMMON WORDY PHRASES

PHRASE	REPLACEMENT
due to the fact that	because
at the present moment	now

has the capability of	can
in a situation in which	when
as a matter of fact	[omit]
in my opinion	[omit]

All-purpose words. These sound serious, yet words like *factor, aspect, situation, type, field, kind,* and *nature* are often fillers, as are modifiers like *very, totally, major, great, really, definitely,* and *absolutely.*

WORDY   Young Goodman Brown is so **totally** overwhelmed by **his own** guilt that he becomes **extremely** suspicious of the people **all** around him. [22 words]

CUT   Young Goodman Brown is so overwhelmed by guilt that he becomes suspicious of the people around him. [17 words]

REWRITTEN   Young Goodman Brown's **overwhelming** guilt makes him **suspect everyone**. [9 words]

Redundant expressions. Redundant pairs (*each and every*) and phrases (*large in size*) say the same thing twice. Eliminate them.

WORDY   Because it was **sophisticated in nature** and **tolerant in style,** Kublai Khan's administration aided China's development in the 1200s.

CUT   Because it was **sophisticated and tolerant,** Kublai Khan's administration aided China's development in the 1200s.

REWRITTEN   Kublai Khan's **adept and tolerant administration** aided China's development in the 1200s.

26b Editing for conciseness

Edit expressions and patterns that lead to wordiness.

STRATEGY **Vary your cutting and trimming.**

- Cut or rewrite what you've already stated or clearly implied.
- Reduce writer's commentary ("In my paper, I will show . . .).
- Compress or delete word groups beginning with *which, who, that,* and *of* by converting clauses to phrases, phrases to words.

CLAUSES	Chavez Park, **which is an extensive facility in the center of town,** was named after Cesar Chavez, **who fought for migrant farmers' rights.**
PHRASES	Chavez Park, **an extensive facility in the center of town,** was named after Cesar Chavez, **an advocate for migrant farmers.**
WORDS	Chavez Park, **a downtown facility,** was named after **migrant advocate** Cesar Chavez.

- Highlight the key points in a passage that interprets or draws conclusions. Combine them as you drop remaining generalities; then add specific supporting detail.

WORDY	**Glaciers** were of central importance in the **shaping of the North American landscape.** Among the many remnants of glacial activity are **deeply carved valleys** and **immense piles of sand and rock.**
COMBINED	Glaciers carved deep valleys and left behind immense piles of sand and rock, shaping much of the North American landscape.
DETAILED	Glaciers carved deep valleys and left behind immense piles of sand and rock, shaping much of the North American landscape in the process. **Cape Cod and Long Island are piles of gravel deposited by glaciers.**

27 | Language Choices

Every speaker of English uses a particular variety of the language—a **dialect**—shaped by region, culture, and home community.

HOME VARIETY	Miss Brill **know** that the lovers **making** fun of her, but she **act** like she **don't** care.
EDITED	Miss Brill **knows** that the lovers **are making** fun of her, but she **acts as if** she **doesn't** care.

In the communities where they're used, these varieties seem natural. In academic, work, and public settings, however, such variations are generally seen as "errors."

27a Recognizing and editing language varieties

A "rule" in one dialect may break a rule in another. In all language, the rules are structures and conventions that people in a group agree, unconsciously, to use. By **code-shifting,** you can substitute "standard edited American English" for your home language variety when you write a college essay, a letter to an official, or a company report.

STRATEGY Look for "rules" in your home language.

Rule in KY: Rule elsewhere:
The lawn needs mowed.   The lawn needs <u>to be</u> mowed.

27b Recognizing and editing disrespectful language

Treat others fairly by eliminating sexist and discriminatory language. Avoid using *mankind* or *men* for humankind and words implying men in occupations (*firemen*). To replace *he, his,* or *him* for all people, try a plural construction (e.g., *their* for *his* rather than *his and hers*).

SEXIST	Every trainee brought **his** laptop with **him.**
AWKWARD	Every trainee brought **his or her** laptop with **him or her.**
BETTER	All trainees brought **their** laptops with **them.**

STRATEGY Watch for stereotyped roles.

STEREOTYPED	The OnCall Pager is **smaller than most doctors' wallets** and **easier to answer than phone calls from their wives.**
	READER'S REACTION: I'm a woman doctor, and I'm insulted. OnCall will never sell a pager in my office!
EDITED	The OnCall Pager **will appeal to doctors because it's small and easy to operate.**

Most readers won't tolerate unfair biases against groups of people.

DEMEANING	My paper focuses on the **weird** courtship rituals of a **barbaric** Aboriginal tribe in southwestern Australia.
	READER'S REACTION: Your paper sounds biased. How can you treat this topic fairly if you don't respect the tribe?
EDITED	My paper focuses on the unique courtship rituals of an Aboriginal tribe in southwestern Australia.

SECTION 6
Writing with Conventions

Voices from the Community

" Punctuation should be governed by its function, which is to make the author's meaning clear, to promote ease of reading, and in varying degrees to contribute to the author's style. **"**

The Chicago Manual of Style, 14th ed.

28 Commas

Because a comma can join, separate, or disrupt, it's easy to misuse.

CONFUSING   During the study interviews were used to gather responses
              from participants, and to supplement written artifacts.
              READER'S REACTION: I can't tell where ideas begin and end.

28b
∧
,

EDITED   During the study , interviews were used to gather responses
              from participants and to supplement written artifacts.

Instead of sprinkling commas at pauses, consider your readers. Public and
work communities that favor direct prose may expect the fewest commas,
while academic readers are likely to expect formal comma usage.

28a Recognizing commas that join sentences

When you use *and, but, or, for, nor, so,* or *yet* (**coordinating conjunctions**) to link two word groups that can stand alone as sentences, place
a comma *before* the conjunction. (Avoid a comma splice. See 16a.)

DRAFT   The rain soaked the soil and the mud buried the road.

EDITED   The rain soaked the soil , **and** the mud buried the road.

28b Editing commas that join sentences

Readers react more strongly if you omit a conjunction than a comma, but
in formal texts they'll see both as errors. Even to join short main clauses,
a comma is always acceptable but might be omitted informally.

STRATEGY **Analyze the pair joined by a conjunction.**

If you find main clauses that could stand alone before and after the conjunction, add a comma *before* the conjunction.

Apex tried to ship the order**,** **but** the truck was late.

If you find any other sentence element before or after the conjunction, do *not* separate the pair with a comma.

PAIR SPLIT	We sanded**,** and stained the old table.
EDITED	We **sanded** and **stained** the old table.
PAIR SPLIT	I used stain that was cheap**,** and easy to clean.
EDITED	I used stain that was **cheap** and **easy to clean.**

28c
,

28c Recognizing commas that set off sentence elements

The simplest sentences need no comma.

noun phrase	verb phrase
The storm	developed quickly.

You may add a layer to the beginning with an **introductory expression** or interrupt a sentence with **parenthetical expressions** or **nonrestrictive modifiers** that add interesting detail. Set these off with commas.

INTRODUCTORY	**For nearly an hour,** the rain drenched Old Town.
TRANSITION	**In addition,** the hail caused damage.
INTERRUPTER	It broke**,** **I think,** a dozen church windows.

CONJUNCTIVE ADVERB	We hope **,** **therefore** **,** that someone starts a repair fund.
TAG QUESTION	We'll contribute **,** **won't we?**
CONTRAST	The windows' beauty touches all of us **,** **not just the church members.**
DIRECT ADDRESS	Recall **,** **friends of beauty** **,** that every gift helps.
NONRESTRICTIVE MODIFIER	The stained glass **,** **glowing like exotic jewels** **,** enriches us all.

28d   Editing commas that set off sentence elements

Use two commas to enclose an expression in mid sentence; use just one after an opening or before a closing expression.

Introductory elements.   Readers expect a comma to signal where the introduction ends and the main sentence begins.

STRATEGY Set off introductory wording for readability.

| CONFUSING | Forgetting to alert the media before the rally Jessica rushed to the park. |
| EDITED | Forgetting to alert the media before the rally **,** Jessica rushed to the park. |

In general, put a comma after a long introductory element following a subordinating conjunction (*although, because, when*; see 25b), a preposition (*during, without*; see 224-R), or a verbal (see 217-R). Also add a comma if a short introductory element might confuse readers.

| CONFUSING | By six boats began showing up. |
| EDITED | By six **,** boats began showing up. |

Parenthetical expressions. Use commas to help readers identify word groups that interrupt a sentence.

DRAFT   Teams should meet even spontaneously as needed.

EDITED   Teams should meet **,** even spontaneously **,** as needed.

Nonessential, nonrestrictive modifiers. Midsentence modifiers act as adjectives or adverbs, adding detail that qualifies other words.

STRATEGY Test whether a modifier is essential.

Drop the modifier, and see whether the essential meaning of the sentence stays the same. If it does, even if it's less informative, the modifier is **nonrestrictive,** adding detail that's interesting or useful but not necessary for meaning. Set it off *with* commas so readers see it as nonessential.

28d
^

DRAFT   Their band **which performs in small clubs** has gotten
                 fine reviews.
                 **TEST: Their band has gotten fine reviews. [The meaning is
                 the same though it's less informative.]**

COMMAS ADDED   Their band **,** **which performs in small clubs,** has
(NONRESTRICTIVE) gotten fine reviews.

If dropping a modifier eliminates essential information and changes the meaning of the sentence, the modifier is **restrictive**. Add it *without* commas so readers see it as a necessary part of the sentence.

DRAFT   The charts **,** **drawn by hand,** were hard to read.
                 **TEST: The charts were hard to read. [This says *all* the charts
                 were hard to read but means that only *some* were.]**

COMMAS OMITTED   The charts **drawn by hand** were hard to read.
(RESTRICTIVE)

Who, which, and *that.* Add commas to set off nonrestrictive (non-essential) clauses beginning with *who, which, whom, whose, when,* or *where.* Because *that* can specify, rather than add, use it in restrictive (essential) clauses. *Which* often adds nonessentials but can be used either way.

NONRESTRICTIVE	Preventive dentistry **,** **which is receiving great emphasis,** may reduce visits to the dentist's office.
RESTRICTIVE	Dentists **who encourage good oral hygiene** often supply helpful advice.
RESTRICTIVE	They also provide sample products **that encourage preventive habits**.

Appositives. An **appositive**, a noun or pronoun that renames a preceding noun, is usually nonrestrictive (nonessential). If so, add commas.

NONRESTRICTIVE	Amy Nguyen **,** **a poet from Vietnam,** published another collection of verse.
RESTRICTIVE	The well-known executive **Louis Gerstner** went from RJR Nabisco to IBM.

28e
∧

28e Editing disruptive commas

Unless you need to set off an intervening expression, you'll irritate readers if a comma separates subject and predicate.

STRATEGY **Drop extra commas between subject and verb.**

SPLIT SUBJECT AND PREDICATE	The painting *Rocks at L'Estaque* **,** is in the Museu de Arte.
EDITED	The **painting** *Rocks at L'Estaque* **is** in the Museu de Arte.

Subordinating conjunctions (see 25b) shouldn't be followed by commas because they introduce entire clauses. Don't mistake them for conjunctive adverbs (such as *however*, see 25a) or transitional expressions (such as *for example*), which should be set off with commas.

> **STRATEGY** Omit commas right after words like *because*.
>
> **EXTRA COMMA**   Although, Jewel lost her luggage, she had her laptop.
> **EDITED**   **Although** Jewel lost her luggage, she had her laptop.

28f   Editing commas with words in a series

Use commas to separate or relate items in a series.

Series of three or more. To avoid ambiguity, consistently use commas between all items of roughly equal status. If an item has multiple parts, place a comma after the entire unit.

> The Human Relations Office has forms for medical benefits, dental and vision options, **and** retirement contributions.

Although readers in the academic community frequently expect the comma just before *and*, it's often omitted, especially in a short, clear list.

Numbered or lettered list. Punctuate a list in a sentence like a series; when items contain commas, separate them with semicolons (see 29c).

> You should (a) measure the water's salinity, (b) weigh any waste in the filter, and (c) determine the amount of dissolved oxygen.

Adjectives in sequence. When you use **coordinate adjectives**, each modifies the noun (or pronoun) on its own. Separate them with commas to show their equal application to the noun. When you use **noncoordinate adjectives**, one modifies the other, and it, in turn, modifies the noun (or pronoun). Don't separate these adjectives with a comma.

STRATEGY Ask questions about adjectives.

If you answer one of these questions with *yes*, the adjectives are coordinate. Separate them with a comma.

- Can you place *and* or *but* between the adjectives?

    COORDINATE
    (EQUAL)   Irrigation has turned dry, infertile [*dry and infertile?—yes*] land into orchards.

    NOT COORDINATE The funds went to new computer [*new and computer?—no*] equipment.

- Is the sense the same if you reverse the adjectives?

    COORDINATE
    (EQUAL)   We left our small, cramped [*cramped small?—yes, the same*] office.

    NOT COORDINATE We bought a red brick [*brick red?—no, could mean a color*] building.

28f
∧
,

COMMA CONVENTIONS

DATES

May 3, 1999   on Monday, June 23,   on July 4, 1776,
5 April 1973   October 2001   fall 2002   June 3

NUMBERS

1,746 sheep (or 1746 sheep) $8,543,234   page 2054

ADDRESSES AND PLACE NAMES IN SENTENCES

in Chicago   in Chicago, Illinois, during May
Fredelle Seed Brokers, Box 389, Holland, MI 30127

PEOPLE'S NAMES AND TITLES

Shamoon, Linda   Cris Burk, A.I.A., was the designer.

OPENINGS AND CLOSINGS OF LETTERS

PERSONAL   Dear Nan,   Dear Soccer Team,   Regards,
BUSINESS OR FORMAL Dear Ms. Yun: Sincerely,

29 | Semicolons and Colons

Semicolons and colons help readers make connections.

TWO SENTENCES   On April 12, 1861, one of Beauregard's batteries fired on Fort **Sumter** • **The** Civil War had begun.

> **READER'S REACTION: These sentences may present facts or drama, but they don't *necessarily* connect events.**

SEMICOLON   On April 12, 1861, one of Beauregard's batteries fired on Fort **Sumter** ; **the** Civil War had begun.

> **READER'S REACTION: The semicolon encourages me to link the battery firing to the Civil War beginning.**

COLON   On April 12, 1861, one of Beauregard's batteries fired on Fort **Sumter** : **the** Civil War had begun.

> **READER'S REACTION: Now I see the guns' firing as a dramatic moment: the beginning of the Civil War.**

You can use semicolons and colons to relate your ideas and to encourage readers to take different perspectives.

29a Recognizing semicolons that join sentences

A semicolon can dramatically highlight a close relationship or a contrast as it creates a brief pause.

TWO SENTENCES   Demand for paper is at an all-time high • Business alone consumes millions of tons each year.

ONE SENTENCE WITH SEMICOLON   Demand for paper is at an all-time high ; business alone consumes millions of tons each year.

29b Editing semicolons that join sentences

When you use a semicolon alone to link main clauses, you assume readers can figure out how the clauses relate. When you add words, you specify the connection for readers.

Assertion **;** ⟶ transition **,** ⟶ assertion
I like apples **;** **however ,** I hate pears.

You can choose a **conjunctive adverb** (*thus, moreover;* see 25a) or a **transitional expression** (*for example, in contrast, on the other hand*). Vary the punctuation depending on where you place such wording.

BETWEEN CLAUSES Joe survived the flood **;** **however ,** Al was never found.
WITHIN CLAUSE Joe survived the flood **;** Al **,** **however ,** was never found.
AT END OF CLAUSE Joe survived the flood **;** Al was never found **,** **however**.

STRATEGY Test both sides of the semicolon.

A semicolon joins main clauses that could stand on their own as sentences. Sometimes, elements in a second clause can be deleted if they "match" elements in the first clause even though the second couldn't stand alone.

ELEMENTS INCLUDED In winter, the **hotel guests enjoy** a roaring log fire **;** in summer, **the hotel guests enjoy** the patio by the river.
ELEMENTS OMITTED In winter, the **hotel guests enjoy** a roaring log fire **;** in summer, the patio by the river.

29c Editing semicolons in a complex series

When items in a series contain commas, readers may have trouble deciding which commas separate parts of the series and which belong within items. To avoid confusion, put semicolons between such items.

I met Debbie Rios, the attorney **;** Rhonda Marron, the accountant **;** and the new financial director.

29d Recognizing and editing colons

A colon effectively joins main clauses when the second clause focuses, sums up, or illustrates the first.

**COLON WITH
MAIN CLAUSES**   The blizzard swept the prairie **:** the Oregon Trail was closed.

The words *before* the colon generally form a complete sentence while those after—the example, list, or quotation—may or may not.

COLON WITH LIST   The symptoms are as follows **:** cough, fever, and pain.

When you introduce a list with a word group other than a complete sentence, do not use a colon.

DRAFT   Her pastimes were **:** walking, volunteering, and cooking.

EDITED   Her pastimes **were walking**, volunteering, and cooking.

EDITED   **She had three pastimes:** walking, volunteering, and cooking.

Whether a quotation is integrated with your words or set off as a block (see 10b), a sentence must precede a colon. If not, use a comma.

**COLON WITH
QUOTATION**   Dan answered his critics **:** "Sales are up and costs down."

COLON CONVENTIONS

Web Site Design **:** *A Beginner's Guide*   John 8 **:** 21–23

"Diabetes **:** Are You at Risk?"   http **:**//www.nytimes.com

10 **:** 32 a.m.   Dear Ms. Will **:** (business letter)   a ratio of 2 **:** 3

29d
:

30 | Apostrophes

Like the dot above the *i*, the apostrophe may seem trivial, but without it, readers would stumble over your text.

MISUSED OR **LEFT OUT**	Though its an 1854 novel, Dickens *Hard Times* remain's an ageless critique of education by fact's. **READER'S REACTION: I can't tell possessives from contractions and plurals in this sentence.**
EDITED	Though it**'**s an 1854 novel, Dickens**'s** *Hard Times* **remains** an ageless critique of education by **facts**.

In all three communities, readers see apostrophes as conventional, not flexible. Check carefully for them.

30a Recognizing apostrophes that mark possession

Nouns that express ownership are called **possessive nouns**. Mark them to distinguish them from plurals.

APOSTROPHE MISSING	The cats meow is becoming fainter. **READER'S REACTION: I expected "The cats meow all night."** **Do you mean many cats or the meow of one cat?**
APOSTROPHE ADDED	The **cat's** meow is becoming fainter.

STRATEGY Test nouns for possession.

If you can turn a noun into a phrase using *of,* use a possessive form. If not, use a plural.

DRAFT	The officers reports surprised the reporters. **TEST: The reports *of* the officers? [*yes, possessive*]** **TEST: Surprised *of* the reporters? [*no, plural*]**
EDITED	The officers**'** reports surprised the reporters.

30b Editing apostrophes that mark possession

Decide what to add: ' + -s or just '.

STRATEGY Check the ending of the noun.

- **Does the noun end in a letter other than -s? Add ' + s.**

  Ohio**'s** taxes   the dog**'s** collar   women**'s** track

- **Does the noun end in -s, and is it plural? Add '.**

  the Solomon**s'** car   buse**s'** routes

- **Does the noun end in -s, and is it singular?**

OPTION #1 (PREFERRED)	Add ' + -s: Chri**s's** van
OPTION #2	Add ' *after* the final -s: Chris**'** van

- **Does the noun end in -s and sound awkward?**

OPTION #1	Hodges**'s** (sounds awkward as "Hodges-es") Add ' but no -s: Hodges**'** (shows one -s sound)
OPTION #2	Change the construction.
DRAFT	the Adams County Schools**'s** policy
EDITED	the policy of the Adams County Schools

Decide whether nouns joined by *and* or *or* act separately or together.

SEPARATE LAWYERS	Bo**'s** and Hal**'s** lawyers are ruthless.
SINGLE LEGAL TEAM	Bo and Hal**'s** lawyers are ruthless.

Omit unnecessary apostrophes in other words that end in -s.

VERB (NOT NOUN)	The staff **orders** supplies early.
PERSONAL PRONOUNS	If **your** car is here, why take **hers**?

30b
∨

APOSTROPHE CONVENTIONS

Dates the ⁹90s the class of ⁹05 1980s

Plural Letters and Numbers p⁹s and q⁹s size 10⁹s

Abbreviations IQs TAs

Dialect I'm **a-goin**⁹ for some **o**⁹ them shrimp.

Hyphenated Noun My **father-in-law**⁹s library is huge.

Multiword Noun The **union leaders**⁹ talks collapsed.

30c Recognizing apostrophes that mark contractions

Informally, use an apostrophe to mark omitted letters when words are combined in a **contraction** (can't = can + not). In most academic writing, avoid splicing nouns with *is* (Zorr's testing = Zorr is testing).

30d Editing apostrophes that mark contractions

Some confusing contractions sound like other words.

they're = they + are   there = adverb

who's = who + is   whose = possessive pronoun

STRATEGY Expand contractions to test the form.

DRAFT **Its** the best animal shelter in **its** area.

EXPANSION TEST: *It is* [*yes, a fit*] the best animal shelter in *it is* [*no, not a fit*] area.

EDITED **It⁹s** the best animal shelter in **its** area.

31 | Quotation Marks

Quotation marks set off someone else's spoken or written words.

DRAFT "Without the navigator," the pilot said, we would have crashed.

READER'S REACTION: Without quotation marks, I didn't realize that the pilot said the last part, too.

EDITED "Without the navigator," the pilot said, "we would have crashed."

Readers in academic, work, and public communities expect you to position quotation marks to show who said what.

31a Recognizing marks that set off quotations

When you quote *directly,* use double quotation marks (" ") around the exact words quoted. (See 10b and 33b.) In dialogue, use new marks and indent when a new person speaks.

DIRECT QUOTATION (SPOKEN) "The loon can stay under water for several minutes," the ranger told us.

DIRECT QUOTATION (WRITTEN) Gross argues that "every generation scorns its offspring's culture" (9).

DIRECT QUOTATION INTERRUPTED "Every generation," so Gross claims, "scorns its offspring's culture" (9).

ESL ADVICE: Quotation Marks

Check for American conventions if your native language uses other marks for quotations or if you are used to British conventions. Search for these marks with your computer to spot unconventional usage.

31b Editing marks that set off quotations

When one quotation contains another, use single marks (' ') for the inside quotation and double marks (" ") for the one enclosing it.

| QUOTATION INSIDE QUOTATION | De Morga's account described the battle that **"**caused his ship to **'**burst asunder**' "** (Goddio 37). |

For quotation marks for emphasis, see 32b. For *indirect* quotations that paraphrase or sum up someone's words, omit quotation marks. (See 10d.)

| PARAPHRASE (INDIRECT) | The pilot credited the navigator with the safe landing. |

| SUMMARY (INDIRECT) | Gross believes that, after just one generation, the social consequences of a major war nearly vanish (5). |

STRATEGY Combine marks in sequence.

- Position commas to help readers distinguish your introduction, commentary, or source from the quotation.

  "Our unity **,**" said the mayor **,** "is our strength."

- If your words end with *that*, don't include a comma.

  Some claimed that "calamity followed Jane." Jane replied that she simply outran it.

- Place these marks *inside* concluding single or double quotation marks: commas, periods, and question or exclamation marks that apply to the quoted material. Place these marks *outside:* semicolons, colons, and question or exclamation marks that apply to the whole sentence.

31c Editing quotation marks with titles of short works

Use quotation marks for titles of short works, parts of larger works, and unpublished works.

31c
" "

CONVENTIONS FOR TITLES

ITALICS OR UNDERLINING	QUOTATION MARKS
BOOK, NOVEL, COLLECTION *The Labyrinth of Solitude* *The White Album*	**CHAPTER, ESSAY, SELECTION** "The Day of the Dead" "Once More to the Lake"
PAMPHLET *Guide for Surgery Patients*	**SECTION** "Anesthesia"
LONG POEM *Paradise Lost* *The One Day*	**SHORT POEM, FIRST LINE TITLE** "Richard Cory" "Whoso list to hunt"
RADIO, TV PROGRAM *The West Wing* *20/20*	**EPISODE, REPORT** "Gone Quiet" "Daycare Dilemmas"
MUSICAL WORK, ALBUM *Messiah* *Invisible Touch* *Organ Symphony* BUT Symphony no. 3 in C Minor, op. 78	**SECTION, SONG** "All We Like Sheep" "Big Money"
MAGAZINE, NEWSPAPER *Discover* the *Denver Post*	**ARTICLE** "What Can Baby Learn?" "Asbestos Found in Schools"
SCHOLARLY JOURNAL *Composition Review*	**ARTICLE** "Student Revision Practices"
PLAY, FILM, ART WORK *King Lear* *Winged Victory*	**UNPUBLISHED WORK, LECTURE** "Renaissance Women" "Sources of Heroic Ballads"

> NO ITALICS, UNDERLINING, OR QUOTATION MARKS
>
> **SACRED BOOKS, PUBLIC OR LEGAL DOCUMENTS**
>
> Bible, Koran, Talmud, United States Constitution
>
> **TITLE OF YOUR OWN PAPER (UNLESS PUBLISHED)**
>
> The Theme of the Life Voyage in Crane's "Open Boat"
>
> The Role of Verbal Abuse in <u>The Color Purple</u>

32a
ital/
und

32 | Italics and Underlining

Type that slants to the right—italic type—emphasizes words and ideas. In handwritten or typed texts, <u>underlining</u> is its equivalent: <u>The Color Purple</u> = *The Color Purple*.

UNDERLINING   Alice Walker's novel <u>The Color Purple</u> has been praised and criticized since 1982.

   READER'S REACTION: I can spot the title right away.

Some readers, including many college teachers, prefer underlining because it's easy to see. Observe your community's conventions.

32a Recognizing conventions for italics (underlining)

Italicize titles of most long, complete works (see 31c). Italicize names of specific ships, planes, trains, and spacecraft (*Voyager VI, Orient Express*) but not *types* of vehicles (Boeing 767) or *USS* and *SS* (USS *Corpus Christi*). Italicize uncommon foreign expressions (*omertà*) but not common ones (junta, taco). Italicize scientific names for plants (*Chrodus crispus*) and animals (*Gazella dorcas*) but not common names (seaweed, gazelle).

32b Editing for conventions for emphasis

Use italics to focus on a term or a word, letter, or number as itself.

In Boston, *r* is pronounced *ah* so that *car* becomes *cah*.

Set off technical or unusual terms with quotation marks or italics.

In real estate, "FSBO" (pronounced "fizbo") refers to a home that is "for sale by owner."

You can—*sparingly*—use italics for emphasis or contrast or use quotation marks for irony, sarcasm, or distance from a term.

STRATEGY **Rewrite to eliminate excessive emphasis.**

In personal and informal writing, underlining may add "oral" emphasis.

INFORMAL   Hand the receipts to me.

MORE FORMAL   Give the receipts to me personally.

33 | Capitals

Readers expect capital letters to signal the start of sentences or to identify specific people, places, and things.

CAPITALS MISSING   thanks, ahmed, for your file. i'll review it by tuesday.

   READER'S REACTION: Email or not, missing capitals are distracting.

CAPITALS IN PLACE   Thanks, Ahmed, for your file. I'll review it by Tuesday.

Follow capitalization conventions to make reading easy.

33a Recognizing capitals that begin sentences

Capital letters begin both sentences and partial sentences (see 15c).

> **P**ack for Yellowstone this July. **W**ildlife and wonders galore!

33b Editing capitals that begin sentences

When capitals are flexible, be consistent within a text.

STRATEGY Adjust your capitals when you quote.

Especially in the academic community, capitalize the first word in a quotation that is a complete sentence or that begins your sentence.

| SENTENCE QUOTED | According to Galloway, "**T**he novel opens with an unusual chapter" (18). |

Don't capitalize part of a quotation integrated into your sentence structure or interrupted by your own words.

| INTEGRATED | Galloway notes that the book "**o**pens with an unusual chapter" (18). |
| INTERRUPTED | "**T**he novel," claims Galloway, "**o**pens with an unusual chapter" (18). |

Sentence in parentheses. Capitalize the first word of a sentence that stands on its own, but not one placed *inside* another sentence.

| FREESTANDING | By this time, the Union forces were split into nineteen sections. (**E**ven so, Grant was determined to unite them.) |
| ENCLOSED | Saskatchewan depends on farming (**t**he province produces over half of Canada's wheat), oil, and mining. |

First word in a line of poetry. Traditionally, lines of poetry begin with capitals, but follow the poet's practice.

We said goodbye at the barrier,

And she slipped away. . . .

> Robert Daseler, "At the Barrier," *Levering Avenue*

Questions in a series. Capitalize or lowercase the series.

OPTION #1　　　　Do we need posters? **S**igns? **F**lyers?

OPTION #2　　　　Do we need posters? **s**igns? **f**lyers?

Sentence after a colon. If a *sentence* follows a colon, choose capitals
or lowercase. Otherwise, do not use a capital.

OPTION #1　　　　The province is bilingual: **O**ne-third speak French and
　　　　　　　　　the rest English.

OPTION #2　　　　The province is bilingual: **o**ne-third speak French and
　　　　　　　　　the rest English.

Run-in list. When items in a list are not presented on separate lines,
don't capitalize word groups or sentences.

NOT CAPITALIZED　　Include costs for (a) **l**abs, (b) **p**hones, and (c) **s**upplies.

Vertical list. Capitalize sentences in vertical lists. Choose whether to
capitalize word groups in an outline without periods.

OPTION #1	OPTION #2
1. **L**ab facilities	1. **l**ab facilities
2. **E**quipment	2. **e**quipment

33c Editing capitals that begin words

Capitalize names of specific people, places, and things **(proper nouns)**
as well as related **proper adjectives**.

　　Brazil, Dickens　　　　Brazilian music, Dickensian plot

33c
cap

33c
cap

CAPITALIZATION CONVENTIONS

CAPITALS	LOWERCASE
INDIVIDUALS, RELATIVES	
Georgia O'Keeffe, Mother	my cousin, her dad
PEOPLE, LANGUAGES	
Maori, African American	the language, the people
TIME PERIODS, SEASONS	
October, Ramadan	spring, winter, holiday
RELIGIONS, RELATED SUBJECTS	
Talmud, Bible, God	talmudic, biblical, a god
ORGANIZATIONS, INSTITUTIONS, MEMBERS	
U.S. Senate	a senator
Air Line Pilots Association	the union, a union member
PLACES, RESIDENTS, GEOGRAPHIC REGIONS	
Malaysia, the Southwest	the country, southwestern
BUILDINGS, MONUMENTS	
Taj Mahal, Getty Museum	the tower, a bridge
HISTORICAL PERIODS, EVENTS, MOVEMENTS	
Jazz Age, Postmodernism	the movement, a trend
ACADEMIC INSTITUTIONS, COURSES	
Harbor Community College	a university, the college
Sociology 203, Art 101	a philosophy course
COMPANY NAMES, TRADE NAMES, VEHICLES	
Siemens, Kleenex, Voyager	the company, tissues, van
SCIENTIFIC, TECHNICAL, MEDICAL TERMS	
Big Dipper, Earth (planet)	star, earth (ground)

In titles, capitalize first and last words, and all words between *except* articles (*a, an, the*), prepositions under five letters (*of, to*), and coordinating conjunctions (*and, but*). Capitalize the word after any colon.

The Mill on the Floss   "Civil Rights: What Now?"

Building a Small Business (your own title)

For APA references, capitalize only proper nouns and the first letters of titles and subtitles of full works (see 12b).

34 | Abbreviations

When they are accepted by both writer and reader, abbreviations act as a kind of shorthand, making a sentence easy to write and read.

CONFUSING   **Jg • Rich • Par was a U of C law prof •**

READER'S REACTION: What is "U of C"—the University of California?

CLEAR   **Judge Richard Par was a University of Chicago law professor.**

Try to aid readers, not baffle them with inappropriate abbreviations.

34a Recognizing and editing abbreviations

Titles with proper names. Abbreviate a title just before or after a person's name. Use one form of a title at a time.

Jack Gill, **Sr •**   **Dr •** Vi McGee   Vi McGee, **D • D • S •**

ESL ADVICE: Abbreviated Titles

If titles such as *Dr.* or *Mrs.* do not require periods in your first language as they do in English, proofread carefully.

Spell out the title if it's *part of your reference to the person* or if does not appear next to a proper name.

Professor Drew   Prof. Ann Drew   NOT Prof. Drew

Exceptions: Rev. Mills   Dr. Smith

Abbreviated academic titles such as *M.A., Ph.D., B.S.,* and *M.D.* can be used on their own or follow a name.

People and organizations. Readers accept abbreviations that are familiar (IBM), simple (AFL-CIO), or standard in context (FAFSA). Most use capitals without periods.

<table>
<tr><td>**Organizations**</td><td>NAACP, AMA, GM, CNN, 3M</td></tr>
<tr><td>**Countries**</td><td>USA (*or* U.S.A.), UK (*or* U.K.)</td></tr>
<tr><td>**People**</td><td>JFK, LBJ, FDR, MLK</td></tr>
<tr><td>**Things or Events**</td><td>FM, TB, AWOL, DUI, TGIF</td></tr>
</table>

34a
abbrev

STRATEGY **Introduce an unfamiliar abbreviation.**

Give the full expression when you first use it, and show the abbreviation in parentheses. Then, use just the abbreviation.

The **American Library Association (ALA)** studies policy on information access. The **ALA** also opposes censorship.

Dates and numbers. Abbreviations (\$, no. for number) may be used with *specific* dates, numbers, or amounts.

<table>
<tr><td>A.D. or AD 79</td><td>*anno Domini,* "in the year of Our Lord"</td></tr>
<tr><td>C.E. or CE</td><td>*Common Era* (alternative for A.D.)</td></tr>
<tr><td>55 B.C. or BC</td><td>*before Christ*</td></tr>
<tr><td>B.C.E. or BCE</td><td>*before common era* (alternative for B.C.)</td></tr>
<tr><td>a.m. or A.M.</td><td>*ante meridiem,* "before noon" (A.M. in print)</td></tr>
<tr><td>p.m. or P.M.</td><td>*post meridiem,* "after noon" (P.M. in print)</td></tr>
</table>

34b Editing to use abbreviations sparingly

In research, scientific, technical, or specialized contexts, such as documenting sources, you can abbreviate more than in formal text.

> **CONVENTIONS FOR ABBREVIATIONS**
>
> - **In formal writing**
>
>   Thursday, not Thurs.   Walton Avenue, not Ave.
>
>   *Exception:* 988 Red Road, Paramus, NJ 07652
>
>   physical education   quart   mile   kilogram   chapter
>
>   *Exceptions:* rpm, mph (with or without periods)
>
> - **In tables or graphs:** @, #, =, −, +, other symbols
> - **In documentation:** ch.   p.   pp.   fig.
> - **In documentation and parentheses (from Latin)**
>
>   e.g.: for example (*exempli gratia*)   i.e.: that is (*id est*)
>
>   et al.: and others (*et alii*)   etc.: and so forth (*et cetera*)

35 | Numbers

You can convey numbers with numerals (37, 18.6), words (fifteen, two million), or a combination (7th, 2nd, 25 billion).

GENERAL TEXT	These **fifty-two** chemists represent **thirty** labs.
	READER'S REACTION: In general academic texts, I expect most numbers to be spelled out.
TECHNICAL	These **52** chemists represent **30** labs.
	READER'S REACTION: In technical papers, I expect more figures.

Follow the advice here for numbers in general writing. In technical, business, and scientific contexts, seek advice from a teacher, supervisor, colleague, or style guide about conventional and consistent usage.

CONVENTIONS FOR NUMBERS IN GENERAL TEXT

- **Addresses and Routes**
  Interstate 6   2450 Ridge Road, Alhambra, CA 91801

- **Dates**
  September 7, 1976   1880–1910   from 1955 to 1957
  1960s   the sixties   the '60s (informal)   October seventh
  nineteenth century   A.D. (or C.E.) 980   class of '05

- **Times of Day**
  10:52   6:17 a.m.   12 p.m. (noon)   12 a.m. (midnight)
  four in the morning   four o'clock   half past eight

- **Parts of a Written Work**
  Chapter 12   Genesis 1:1–6 or Gen.1.1–6 (MLA style)
  Macbeth 2.4.25–28 (or act II, scene iv, lines 25–28)

- **Measurements, Fractions, Decimals, Statistics**
  120 MB   55 mph   6'4"   47 psi   21 ml
  7-5/8   27.3   67 percent (or 67%)
  7 out of 10   3 to 1   won 5 to 4   a mean of 23

- **Money**
  $7,883 $4.29 $7.2 million (or $7,200,000)

- **Rounded**
  75 million years   three hundred thousand voters

- **Ranges:** Simply supply the last two figures in the second number unless readers will need more to avoid confusion.
  34–45   95–102 (not 95–02)   370–420   1534–620

- **Ranges of Years:** Supply all digits for different centuries.
  1890–1920   1770–86   476–823   42–38 B.C.

- **Clusters:** items 2, 5, and 8 through 10 (or 8–10)

35a Recognizing when to spell or use numerals

In general, spell out numbers composed of one or two words, treating hyphenated compounds as a single word.

ten books   **twenty-seven** computers   **306** employees

35b Editing numbers in general text

Treat comparable numbers consistently in a passage, either as numerals (used for all if required for one) or as words.

CONSISTENT   Café Luna's menu soon expanded from **85** to **104** items.

STRATEGY Spell out opening numbers, or rewrite.

INAPPROPRIATE   **428** houses are finished.

DISTRACTING   **Four hundred twenty-eight** houses are finished.

EASY TO READ   **In Talcott, 428** houses are finished.

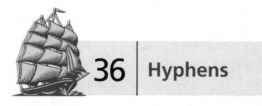

36 | Hyphens

Readers expect hyphens both to join and divide words.

CONFUSING   The Japanese language proposal is well prepared.

        READER'S REACTION: Is the proposal *in* or *about* the Japanese language?

CLARIFIED   The Japanese-language proposal is well prepared.

Type a hyphen as a *single* line (-) with no space on either side: well-trained engineer, not well - trained engineer.

36a Recognizing hyphens that join words

A **compound word** is made from two or more words that may be hyphenated (*double-decker*), spelled as one word (*timekeeper*), or treated as separate words (*letter carrier*). Compounds change rapidly; check a current dictionary. Observe accepted practice in work or public contexts.

36b Editing hyphens that join words

Numbers. In general (not technical) writing, hyphenate numbers between twenty-one and ninety-nine (even if part of a larger one), inclusive numbers, and fractions: *fifty‑one thousand, volumes 9‑14, two‑thirds.*

Prefixes and suffixes. Hyphenate a prefix before a capital or number and with *ex-*, *self-*, *all-*, *-elect*, and *-odd*: *pre‑1989, self‑centered.*

Letters with words. Hyphenate a letter and a word forming a compound, except in music terms: *A‑frame, T‑shirt, A minor, G sharp.*

Confusing words. Use hyphens to help readers distinguish different words with the same spelling *(recreation, re-creation)* or to clarify words with repeated letters *(anti-imperialism, post-traumatic).*

Compound modifiers. When two or more words work as a single modifier, generally hyphenate them *before* but not *after* a noun.

BEFORE NOUN **(-)**   Many **nausea‑inducing** drugs treat cancer.

AFTER NOUN **(NO -)**   Many drugs that treat cancer are **nausea inducing**.

Do not hyphenate *-ly* adverbs (highly regarded staff) or comparative forms (more popular products).

STRATEGY Try suspended hyphens with modifiers.

Reduce repetition with hyphens that signal the suspension of an element until the end of a series of parallel compound modifiers. Leave a space after the hyphen and before *and*, but not before a comma.

The lab uses **oil- and water-based** compounds.

36c Editing hyphens that divide words

Traditionally you could split a word at the end of a line, marking the break *between syllables* with a hyphen. Now word processors automatically hyphenate but often create hard-to-read lines or incorrectly split words. As a result, many writers turn off this feature. When you must divide an electronic address, do so after a slash. Don't add a hyphen.

37 | Spelling

Readers in all communities expect accurate spelling.

INCORRECT   The city will not **except** any late bids.

> **READER'S REACTION: I get annoyed when careless or lazy writers won't correct their spelling!**

PROOFREAD   The city will not **accept** any late bids.

Readers may laugh at a newspaper misspelling but harshly judge a writer who misspells in an academic paper or work document.

37a Using the computer to proofread for spelling

When you use a spelling checker, the computer compares each word in your text with the words in the dictionary in its memory. If it finds a match, it assumes your word is correct. If it does *not* find a match, it asks you if the word is misspelled. What it can't identify are words correctly spelled but used incorrectly such as *lead* for *led*.

37b Recognizing and editing spelling errors

Correct errors you see; ask readers to spot others.

STRATEGY **Go beyond the spelling checker.**

- Say the word carefully. Look up possible spellings, even odd ones. If you reach the right area in a dictionary, you may find the word.
- Try a dictionary for poor spellers that lists correct spellings (*phantom*) and likely misspellings (*fantom*).
- Try a thesaurus; the word may be listed as a synonym.
- Ask others for technical terms; verify their advice in a dictionary.
- Check the indexes of books on the word's topic.
- Look for the word in textbooks, company materials, or newspapers.
- Add a tricky word to your own spelling list. Invent a way to remember it (associating the two *z*'s in *quizzes* with boredom—*zzzzzz*).

37b
spell

Try to identify spelling patterns that will help you improve.

COMMON SPELLING PATTERNS

PATTERNS FOR PLURALS

WORD ENDING	CHANGE	EXAMPLES
most nouns	add *-s*	novel**s**, contract**s**
consonant + *-o*	often add *-es*	potato**es**, hero**es**
	some add *-s*	cello**s**, memo**s**
vowel + *-o*	add *-s*	stereo**s**, video**s**
consonant + *-y*	*y* to *i* + *-es*	gallery ⟶ galler**ies**
proper noun + *-y*	add *-s*	Kennedy ⟶ Kennedy**s**
vowel + *-y*	add *-s*	day**s**, journey**s**, pulley**s**
-f or *-fe*	often *f* to *v* + *-s* or *-es*	life ⟶ li**ves**
		self ⟶ sel**ves**
	some add *-s*	belief**s**, roof**s**, turf**s**
-ch, -s, -ss, -sh, -x, or *-z* (a hiss sound)	most add *-es*	bench**es**, bus**es**, fox**es**, kiss**es**, buzz**es**
one-syllable ending in *-s* or *-z*	many double final consonant	quiz ⟶ qui**zz**es

WORD ENDING	CHANGE	EXAMPLES
foreign roots	follow original language	dat**um** ⟶ dat**a** criteri**on** ⟶ criteri**a**
irregular nouns	last word	foot ⟶ f**ee**t basketball**s**
compound	first word if most important	sister-in-law ⟶ sister**s**-in-law

PATTERNS FOR BEGINNINGS (PREFIXES)

Prefixes do not change the spelling of the root word that follows: *precut, post-traumatic, misspell, unendurable*.

PREFIX FOR *NOT*	COMBINATION	EXAMPLES
im-	with *b, m, p*	**im**patient, **im**balance
in-	with others	**in**correct, **in**adequate

37b
spell

PATTERNS FOR ENDINGS (SUFFIXES)

Suffixes may change the root word or pose other problems.

SUFFIX	CHANGE	EXAMPLES
starts with consonant	keep silent *-e*	fat**e**ful, gentl**e**ness
	exceptions	judgment, truly, argument, ninth
starts with vowel	drop silent *-e*	imaginary, generation, decreasing, definable
	exceptions	notic**e**able, chang**e**able

SUFFIX	COMBINATION	EXAMPLES
-ery	4 common words	station**e**ry (paper), cemet**e**ry, monast**e**ry, millin**e**ry
-ary	most others	station**a**ry (fixed in place), secret**a**ry, prim**a**ry, milit**a**ry
"-seed" sound	most use *-cede*	pre**cede**, re**cede**
	several use *-ceed*	pro**ceed**, suc**ceed**, ex**ceed**
	one uses *-sede*	super**sede**

SUFFIX	COMBINATION	EXAMPLES
-able	add if root stands on own	charit**able,** advis**able**
with *-ee* root	keep *-e*	agree**able**
-ible	add if root can't stand on own	cred**ible,** irreduc**ible**

PATTERNS FOR SEQUENCES OF LETTERS WITHIN WORDS

LETTER GROUP	SEQUENCE	EXAMPLES
ie	*i* before *e* except after *c,* or sounding like *a* as in n**ei**ghbor and w**ei**gh.	bel**ie**ve, gr**ie**f, fr**ie**nd re**ce**ive, dece**i**t
	exceptions	an**cie**nt w**ei**rd, s**ei**ze, for**ei**gn, h**ei**ght, th**ei**r, **ei**ther, n**ei**ther, l**ei**sure

The Glossary also lists **homophones,** different words that sound alike.

COMMONLY CONFUSED WORD PAIRS

WORD	MEANING	WORD	MEANING
all ready	prepared	already	by this time
its	possessive of *it*	it's	*it is*
than	compared with	then	next
their	possessive of *they*	there	in that place
whose	possessive of *who*	who's	*who is*
your	possessive of *you*	you're	*you are*

38 | Other Marks and Conventions

You can use punctuation marks to change the style and sense of your prose and adjust its effects on readers.

DASHES
The boy—**clutching his allowance**—came to the store.
READER'S REACTION: Dashes show strong emphasis; I can tell how hard the boy worked to save his money.

PARENTHESES
The boy (**clutching his allowance**) came to the store.
READER'S REACTION: Parentheses deemphasize his savings, thus giving his arrival more significance.

COMMAS
The boy, **clutching his allowance**, came to the store.
READER'S REACTION: This direct account doesn't emphasize either the savings or the arrival.

Punctuation marks set boundaries, guide readers, and add emphasis.

38a
( )

38a Recognizing and editing parentheses

Parentheses *enclose:* you can't use just one, and readers will interpret whatever falls between the pair as an aside.

When you sign up for Telepick (including Internet access), you will receive an hour of free calls.

When parentheses *inside a sentence* come at the end, punctuate *after* the closing mark. When you enclose a *freestanding sentence*, punctuate *inside* the closing mark.

INSIDE SENTENCE	People on your list get discounts (once they sign up).
SEPARATE SENTENCE	Try Telepick now. (This offer excludes international calls.)

You can use parentheses to mark numbered or lettered lists.

NUMBERED LIST	Fax Harry's Bookstore (555-0934) to (1) order books, (2) inquire about items, or (3) sign up for events.

38b Recognizing and editing dashes

Too many may strike academic readers as informal, but dashes can add flair to work and public appeals, ads, or brochures. Type a dash as two unspaced hyphens, without space before or after: --. A print dash appears as a single line: —. Use one dash with an idea or series that opens or ends a sentence; use a pair to enclose words in the middle.

OPENING LIST	**Extended visiting hours, better meals, and more exercise**--these were the inmates' demands.
PAIR IN THE MIDDLE	For her service to two groups--**Kids First and Food Basket**--Olivia was voted Volunteer of the Year.

STRATEGY Convert excessive dashes to other marks.

Circle dashes that seem truly valuable—maybe marking a key point. Replace others with commas, parentheses, colons, or emphatic wording.

38c Recognizing and editing brackets

Academic readers expect you to use brackets scrupulously (though other readers may find them pretentious). When you add your words to a quotation for clarity or background, bracket this **interpolation**. Also bracket *sic* (Latin for "thus") after a source error to confirm your accuracy.

INTERPOLATION As Walz notes, "When Catholic Europe adopted the new Gregorian calendar in 1582, Protestant England still followed October 4 by October 5 [Julian calendar]" (4).

38d Recognizing and editing ellipses

The **ellipsis** uses three *spaced* periods to mark where something has been left out. Academic readers expect ellipses to mark omissions of irrelevant material from quotations; other readers may prefer full quotations.

> ### CONVENTIONS FOR ELLIPSIS MARKS
>
> - Use three spaced periods . . . for ellipses in a sentence or line of poetry. Bracket the ellipsis [. . .] in MLA style.
> - Use a period before an ellipsis ending a sentence. . . .
> - Leave a space before the first period . . . and after the last unless the ellipsis is bracketed.
> - Omit ellipses when you begin quotations (unless needed for clarity) or use clearly incomplete words or phrases.
> - Retain another punctuation mark before omitted words if needed for the sentence structure; . . . omit it otherwise.
> - Bracket a series of spaced periods (MLA style) to show an omitted line (or more) of poetry in a block quotation.

When you drop *part* of a sentence, maintain normal sentence structure so readers can follow the passage.

INTERVIEW NOTES Museum Director: "We expect the Inca pottery in our special exhibit to attract historians from as far away as Chicago, while the vivid jewelry draws the public."

CONFUSING DRAFT The museum director hopes "the Inca pottery . . . historians . . . vivid jewelry . . . public."

EDITED   The museum director "expect[s] the Inca pottery ● ● ●
                   to attract historians ● ● ● while the vivid jewelry draws
                   the public."

In narrative, ellipses can show a pause or ongoing action.

FOR SUSPENSE   Large paw prints led to the tent● ● ● ●

38e Recognizing and editing slashes

You can use a slash to mark alternatives (the **on/off** switch), especially in
technical documents, but readers may find it informal or imprecise (pre-
ferring *or* instead). When you quote poetry *within* your text, separate
lines of verse with a slash, typing a space before and after.

The speaker in Sidney's sonnet hails the moon: "O Moon, thou
climb'st the skies! **/** How silently . . ." (1–2).

38f Recognizing and editing end marks

Speakers change pitch or pause to mark sentence boundaries. Writers use
symbols—period, question mark, exclamation point.

LESS FORMAL   And why do we need you? You help our lovable pups
                   find new families!
                   **READER'S REACTION: This bouncy style is great for the vol-
                   unteer brochure but not the annual report.**

MORE FORMAL   The League's volunteers remain our most valuable asset,
                   matching abandoned animals with suitable homes.

Readers in all communities expect periods to end sentences. Some readers may accept informal use of question marks and exclamation points.

Periods. All sentences that are *statements* end with periods—even if
they contain embedded clauses that report, rather than ask, questions.

Periods also mark decimal points (5.75) and abbreviations (Dr., Ms., pp., etc., a.m.) though many abbreviations, pronounced as words or by letter, don't require them (NASA, GOP, OH).

Question marks. End a direct question with a question mark, but use a period to end an **indirect question**—a sentence with an embedded clause that asks a question.

DIRECT	When is the train leaving?
DIRECT: QUOTED	Lu asked, "Why is it so hot?"
DIRECT: TWO CLAUSES	Considering that the tax break has been widely publicized, why have so few people filed for a refund?
INDIRECT	Jose asked if we needed help.

Exclamation points. These marks end emphatic statements such as commands or warnings but are rarely used in academic or work writing.

EMPHATIC	Get the campers off the cliff!

STRATEGY **Use draft punctuation to guide your editing.**

Like question marks, exclamation points can be used informally, expressing dismay, shock, or strong interest. Edit for strong words to emphasize.

DRAFT	Rescuers spent hours (!) trying to reach the child.
EDITED	Rescuers spent **agonizing** hours trying to reach the child.

38g Recognizing and editing electronic addresses

When you cite an electronic address, record its characters exactly—including slashes, @ ("at") signs, underscores, colons, and periods.

http://www.access.gpo.gov/su_docs

38h Combining marks

- **Always use marks that enclose in pairs**.

  ( )   [ ]   " "   ' '

  Use commas and dashes in pairs to enclose mid-sentence elements.
  Type a dash as a pair ▬▬ of hyphens.

- **Use multiple marks when each mark plays its own role**. If an
  abbreviation with a period falls in the *middle* of a sentence, the period
  may be followed by another mark, such as a comma, dash, colon, or
  semicolon.

  Experts spoke until 10 **p.m.,** and we left at 11 **p.m.**

- **Eliminate multiple marks when their roles overlap**. When an
  abbreviation with a period concludes a sentence, that one period will
  also end the sentence. Omit a comma *before* mid-sentence parentheses; *after* the parentheses, use whatever mark would otherwise occur.

- **Avoid confusing duplicates**. If items listed in a sentence include
  commas, separate them with semicolons, not more commas.

  If one parenthetical element falls within another, use brackets to enclose the unit inside the parentheses.

  Use one pair of dashes at a time, not dashes within dashes.

Resources for Editing

How can you recognize a sentence?

A **sentence**—also called a **main (or independent) clause**—is a word group that can stand alone. It has a subject and a predicate (a verb and any words that complete it).

SENTENCE   **Hungry bears** <u>were hunting</u> food.

SENTENCE   Because spring snows had damaged many plants, **hungry bears** <u>were hunting</u> food in urban areas.

A **subordinate (or dependent) clause** has a subject and a predicate, yet it cannot stand on its own because it begins with a subordinating word like *because, although, which,* or *that* (see 25b).

FRAGMENT   Because **spring snows** <u>had damaged</u> many plants

A **phrase** is a word group that lacks a subject, a predicate, or both. It cannot stand alone.

FRAGMENT   were hunting   in urban areas   the hungry bears

How can you test for a sentence?

edit

- Ask questions: *Who* (or *what*) *does? Who* (or *what*) *is?*
- Does a word group answer "Who?" or "What?" If not, it lacks a subject and is a fragment.
- Does a word group answer "Does?" or "Is?" If not, then it lacks a verb and is a fragment.
- Can you turn a word group into a question that can be answered *yes* or *no*? If you can, it is a sentence. (Caution: Begin with *did,* not *is, are, have,* or *has,* or you may add a verb to the test group.)
- Is a word group with both a subject and a complete verb controlled by a subordinating word? If so, this word group is not a sentence and must be attached to a main clause.

For examples of these sentence tests, turn to Chapter 15 on fragments. See also Chapter 16 on comma splices and fused sentences.

HOW DO WORDS WORK IN SENTENCES?	
You can recognize	**By looking for words that do this**
nouns	name a person, a place, an idea, or a thing (*Jed, cafeteria, doubt, chair*)
pronouns	take the place of a noun (*them, she, his*)
verbs	express action (*jump, write*), occurrence (*become, happen*), and being (*be, seem*)
adverbs	modify or qualify verbs, adjectives, and other adverbs telling when, where, how, how often, which direction, or what degree (*now, very, quite, too, quickly*)
adjectives	modify or qualify nouns and pronouns, telling how many, what kind, which one, what size, what color, or what shape (*five, many, attractive, blue, young*)
prepositions	add information by linking the noun or pronoun following to the rest of the sentence (*after, at, in, by, on, near, with*)
conjunctions	join other words, signaling their relationships (*and, but, because, though*)
interjections	convey a strong reaction or emotion (*Oh, no! Hey!*)

edit

How do sentence patterns work?

Five basic predicate structures

1. Subject + intransitive verb

The bus crashed.

2. Subject + transitive verb + direct object

A passenger called the police.

3. Subject + transitive verb + indirect object + direct object

The paramedic gave everyone a blanket.

4. Subject + transitive verb + direct object + object complement

Officials found the driver negligent.

5. Subject + linking verb + subject complement

The quick-thinking passenger was a hero.

Four sentence structures

1. A **simple sentence** has one main (independent) clause and no subordinate (dependent) clauses.

The mayor proposed an expansion of city hall.

2. A **compound sentence** has two or more main (independent) clauses and no subordinate (dependent) clauses (see 25a).

main clause   main clause

Most people praised the plan, yet **some found it** dull.

3. A **complex sentence** has one main (independent) clause and one or more subordinate (dependent) clauses (see 25b).

subordinate clause   main clause

Because people objected, **the architect revised the plans**.

4. A **compound-complex sentence** has two or more main (independent) clauses and one or more subordinate (dependent) clauses.

subordinate clause   subordinate clause

Because he wanted to make sure that the expansion did not damage

main clause

the existing building, **the architect examined the older**

main clause

structure, and **he asked the contractor to test the soil stability**.

Four sentence purposes

1. A **declarative sentence** makes a statement: The motor is making a rattling noise.

edit

2. An **interrogative sentence** poses a question: Have you checked it for overheating?
3. An **imperative sentence** requests or commands: Check it again.
4. An **exclamatory sentence** exclaims: It's on fire!

What are the principal parts of verbs?

BASE FORM	PAST	PRESENT PARTICIPLE	PAST PARTICIPLE
REGULAR VERBS			
live	lived	living	lived
IRREGULAR VERBS			
eat	ate	eating	eaten
run	ran	running	run

What are the tenses of verbs in the active voice?

Decide when actions or events occur; then use this chart to help you select the tense you need for a regular (*examine*) or irregular (*begin*) verb.

edit

Present, past, and future (showing simple actions)

Present: action taking place now, including habits and facts occurring all the time

| I/you/we/they | examine/begin |
| he/she/it | examines/begins |

Past: action that has already taken place at an earlier time

| I/you/he/she/it/we/they | examined/began |

Future: action that will take place at an upcoming time

| I/you/he/she/it/we/they | will examine/begin |

Present, past, and future perfect (showing order of events)

Present Perfect: action that has recurred or has continued from the past to the present

I/you/we/they	have examined/begun
he/she/it	has examined/begun

Past Perfect: action that had already taken place before something else happened

I/you/he/she/it/we/they	had examined/begun

Future Perfect: action that will have taken place by the time something else happens

I/you/he/she/it/we/they	will have examined/begun

Present, past, and future progressive (showing action in progress)

Present Progressive: action that is in progress now, at this moment

I	am examining/beginning
you/we/they	are examining/beginning
he/she/it	is examining/beginning

Past Progressive: action that was in progress at an earlier time

I/he/she/it	was examining/beginning
you/we/they	were examining/beginning

Future Progressive: action that will be in progress at an upcoming time

I/you/he/she/it/we/they	will be examining/beginning

Present, past, and future perfect progressive (showing the duration of action in progress)

Present Perfect Progressive: action that has been in progress up to now

I/you/we/they	have been examining/beginning
he/she/it	has been examining/beginning

edit

Past Perfect Progressive: action that had already been in progress before something else happened

I/you/he/she/it/we/they   had been examining/beginning

Future Perfect Progressive: action that will have been in progress by the time something else happens

I/you/he/she/it/we/they   will have been examining/beginning

What are the common helping verbs? [ESL]

Be: *am, is, are, was, were, be, being, been*
Have: *have, has, had*
Do: *do, does, did*
Modals: *could, should, would, ought to, can, may, might, must, shall, will*

Progressive form (using forms of *be*)

PAST	subject + *was/were* + present participle I **was** working in my studio yesterday.
PRESENT	subject + *am/is/are* + present participle I **am** working in my studio right now.
FUTURE	subject + *will* (modal) + *be* + present participle I **will be** working in my studio tomorrow.

ESL

edit

Perfect form (using forms of *have*)

PAST	subject + *had* + past participle I **had** tried to call you before I left.
PRESENT	subject + *have/has* + past participle I **have** tried to call you all day.
FUTURE	subject + *will* (modal) + *have* + past participle I **will have** called you by midnight.

What are common time expressions for present and present progressive verbs? [ESL]

Present tense habitual activities

all the time	every day	often	rarely
always	frequently	sometimes	usually

Present progressive activities in progress

at the moment	this afternoon	this month	this year
right now	this evening	this morning	today

How can you recognize active and passive verbs?

Verbs in the **active voice** appear in sentences in which the doer (or agent) of an action is the subject of the sentence.

ESL

	DOER (SUBJECT)	ACTION (VERB)	GOAL (OBJECT)
ACTIVE	The car	**hit**	the lamppost.
ACTIVE	Dana	**distributed**	the flyers.

edit

A verb in the **passive voice** adds a form of *be* as a helping verb to the past participle form. The subject (or doer) may appear as an object after the word *by* in an optional prepositional phrase. (See 20b.)

	GOAL (SUBJECT)	ACTION (VERB)	[DOER: PREPOSITIONAL PHRASE]
PASSIVE	The lamppost	**was hit**	[by the car].
PASSIVE	The flyers	**were distributed**	[by Dana].

How do conditional statements work? [ESL]

Conditional statements depend on a condition or are imagined. Each type has an *if* clause and a result clause that combine different verb tenses.

Type I: True in the present

- Generally true in the present as a habit or as a fact

  if + subject + <u>present tense</u> **subject + <u>present tense</u>**
  If **I** <u>drive</u> to school every day, **I** <u>get</u> to class on time.

- True in the future as a one-time event

  if + subject + <u>present tense</u> **subject + <u>future tense</u>**
  If **I** <u>drive</u> to school today, **I** <u>will get</u> to class on time.

- Possibly true in the future as a one-time event

  if + subject + <u>present tense</u> **subject + <u>modal + base form verb</u>**
  If **I** <u>drive</u> to school today, **I** <u>may get</u> to class on time.

Type II: Untrue or contrary to fact in the present

if + subject + <u>past tense</u> **subject + _would/could/might_ + <u>base form verb</u>**
If **I** <u>drove</u> to school, **I** <u>would arrive</u> on time.

For Type II, the form of _be_ in the _if_ clause is always _were_.

Type III: Untrue or contrary to fact in the past

ESL

       subject + _would/could/might_ +
if + subject + <u>past perfect tense</u> _have_ + <u>past participle</u>
If **I** <u>had driven</u> to school, **I** <u>would</u> not <u>have been</u> late.

edit

What are verbal phrases?

Three verb parts—participles, gerunds, and infinitives—are known as **verbals**. They can function as nouns, adjectives, or adverbs—but they can never stand alone as verbs.

1. Build **participial phrases** with _-ing_ (present participle) or _-ed/-en_ (past participle) forms, using them as adjectives.

   Few neighbors **attending the meeting** owned dogs.

   They signed a petition **addressed to the mayor**.

2. Build a **gerund phrase** around the *-ing* form (present participle) used as a noun.

Closing the landfill may keep it from **polluting the stream**.

3. Build an **infinitive phrase** around the *to* form, using it as an adjective, adverb, or noun.

He used organic methods **to raise his garden**.

To live in the mountains was his goal.

What are the forms of common irregular verbs?

PRESENT	PAST	PAST PARTICIPLE
arise	arose	arisen
be	was/were	been
bear	bore	borne
begin	began	begun
bite	bit	bitten/bit
blow	blew	blown
break	broke	broken
bring	brought	brought
buy	bought	bought
come	came	come
creep	crept	crept
dive	dived/dove	dived
do	did	done
dream	dreamed/dreamt	dreamt
drink	drank	drunk
drive	drove	driven
eat	ate	eaten
fly	flew	flown
forget	forgot	forgotten
forgive	forgave	forgiven
freeze	froze	frozen
get	got	got/gotten

edit

PRESENT	PAST	PAST PARTICIPLE
give	gave	given
go	went	gone
grow	grew	grown
hang	hung	hung
hide	hid	hidden
know	knew	known
lay	laid	laid
lead	led	led
lie	lay	lain
light	lit	lit
prove	proved	proved/proven
ride	rode	ridden
ring	rang	rung
rise	rose	risen
run	ran	run
see	saw	seen
seek	sought	sought
set	set	set
shake	shook	shaken
sing	sang	sung
sink	sank	sunk
sit	sat	sat
speak	spoke	spoken
spring	sprang	sprung
steal	stole	stolen
strike	struck	struck
swear	swore	sworn
swim	swam	swum
take	took	taken
tear	tore	torn
throw	threw	thrown
wake	woke/waked	woken/waked/woke
wear	wore	worn
write	wrote	written

edit

What are the types of nouns?

Count noun: Names individual items that can be counted: *two chairs, four cups, a hundred beans*

Noncount noun (mass noun): Names material or abstractions that cannot be counted: *flour, water, steel*

Collective noun: Names a unit composed of more than one individual or thing: *group, staff, flock* (see Chapter 18 on agreement)

Proper noun: Names specific people, places, titles, or things (see 33c on capitals): *Ms. Phan, Alabama, Reebok*

Common noun: Names nonspecific people, places, or things (see 33c on capitals): *children, winner, town, company*

How do articles and nouns work together? [ESL]

The **indefinite articles** are *a* or *an*; the **definite article** is *the*.

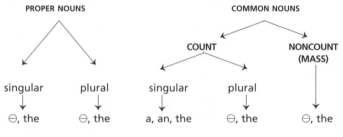

⊖ = no article

Singular proper nouns generally use no article, and **plural proper nouns** usually use *the*.

SINGULAR   Rosa Parks helped initiate the civil rights movement.

PLURAL   **The** Everglades have abundant wildlife.

Singular count nouns cannot stand alone. Use *a* or *an* when you are not referring to any specific person or thing. Use *a* before a consonant sound and *an* before a vowel sound.

ESL

edit

I need **a** car to go to work. [unknown, nonspecific, or any car]

Use *the* when you are referring to an exact, known person or thing.

I need **the** car to go to work. [specific, known car]

Plural count nouns use either no article (to show a generalization) or *the* (to refer to something specific).

GENERALIZATION   Books are the best teachers.

SPECIFIC   **The** books on his desk are due Monday.

Noncount (mass) nouns never use *a* or *an*. They may stand alone (when general) or use *the* (when specific).

GENERAL   Laughter is good medicine.

SPECIFIC   **The** laughter of children is good medicine.

Use *the* when a plural count noun or a noncount noun is followed by a modifier, such as an adjective clause or prepositional phrase, that makes the noun specific.

COUNT   **The** airline tickets that you bought are at half price.

NONCOUNT   **The** information on the flight board has changed.

What do pronouns do?

- **Personal pronouns**: Designate persons or things using a form reflecting the pronoun's role in the sentence (see 19c).

  SINGULAR   *I, me, you, he, him, she, her, it*

  PLURAL   *we, us, you, they, them*

- **Possessive pronouns**: Show ownership (see 30a–b on apostrophes).

  SINGULAR   *my, mine, your, yours, her, hers, his, its*

  PLURAL   *our, ours, your, yours, their, theirs*

- **Relative pronouns**: Introduce subordinate clauses that act as adjectives and answer the questions "What kind of?" and "Which one?"

  who, whom, whose, which, that

- **Interrogative pronouns**: Introduce questions.

  who, which, what

- **Reflexive pronouns**: End in *-self* or *-selves* and enable the subject or doer also to be the receiver of an action.

- **Intensive pronouns**: End in *-self* or *-selves* and add emphasis.

SINGULAR	*myself, yourself, herself, himself, itself*
PLURAL	*ourselves, yourselves, themselves*

- **Demonstrative pronouns**: Point out or highlight an antecedent, refer to a noun or a pronoun, or sum up an entire phrase or clause.

  this, that, these, those

- **Reciprocal pronouns**: Refer to individual parts of a plural antecedent.

  one another, each other

- **Indefinite pronouns**: Refer to people, things, and ideas in general rather than to a specific antecedent. (See the following list.)

edit

What are some indefinite pronouns?

GENERALLY SINGULAR		PLURAL	EITHER SINGULAR OR PLURAL
another	neither	both	all
anybody	nobody	few	any
anyone	none	many	enough
anything	no one	others	more
each	nothing	several	most
either	one	some	
every	other		
everyone	somebody		
everything	someone		
much	something		

What are the forms of comparatives and superlatives?

Adjectives

One syllable: Most add -er and -est (*pink, pinker, pinkest*).
Two syllables: Many add -er and -est; some add either -er and -est
  or *more* and *most* (*foggy, foggier, foggiest; more foggy, most foggy*).
Three (or more) syllables: Add *more* and *most* (*plentiful, more plentiful, most plentiful*).

Adverbs

One syllable: Most add -er and -est (*quick, quicker, quickest*).
Two (or more) syllables: Most add *more* and *most* (*carefully, more
  carefully, most carefully*).

Negative comparisons (adjectives and adverbs)

Use *less* and *least* (*less full, least full; less slowly, least slowly*).

Irregular forms

ADJECTIVE	COMPARATIVE	SUPERLATIVE
bad	worse	worst
good, well (healthy)	better	best
ill (harsh, unlucky)	worse	worst
a little	less	least
many, much, some	more	most
badly, ill (badly)	worse	worst
well (satisfactorily)	better	best

ESL

edit

How do prepositions work? [ESL]
Prepositions of time: *at, on,* and *in*

• Use *at* for a specific time. Use *on* for days and dates. Use *in* for nonspecific times during a day, month, season, or year.

  Brandon was born **at** 11:11 a.m. **on** a Monday **in** 1996.

Prepositions of place: *at, on,* and *in*

* Use *at* for specific addresses. Use *on* for names of streets, avenues, and boulevards. Use *in* for areas of land—states, countries, continents.

  She lives **on** Town Avenue but works **at 99 Low Street in** Dayton.

  Arrange prepositional phrases in this order: place, then time.

  The runners will start **in the park** <u>on Saturday</u>.

To or no preposition to express going to a place

* When you express the idea of going to a place, use the preposition *to*.

  I am going **to** work.   I am going **to** the office.

* In some cases, use no preposition: I am going home.

For and *since* in time expressions

ESL

* Use *for* with an amount of time (minutes, hours, days, months, years) and *since* with a specific date or time.

  The housing program has operated **for** many years, **since** 1971.

edit

Prepositions with nouns, verbs, and adjectives

* Nouns, verbs, and adjectives may appear with certain prepositions.

  NOUN + PREPOSITION   He has an <u>understanding</u> **of** global politics.

  VERB + PREPOSITION   Managers <u>worry</u> **about** many things.

What are some common prepositions?

about	along	behind
above	among	below
across	around	beneath
after	as	between
against	at	beyond

by	like	through
concerning	near	to
despite	of	toward
down	off	under
during	on	until
except	out	up
for	outside	with
from	over	within
in	past	

Credits *(continued from p. vi)*

Michael Gregor, "Milk . . . Help Yourself," *AnimaLife,* Fall 1994, Vol. 5, No.1. Reprinted by permission of the publisher. **Donald Hall**, "A Small Fig Tree," from *Old and New Poems.* Copyright © 1990 by Donald Hall. Reprinted by permission of Ticknor Fields/Houghton Mifflin Co. All rights reserved. **Maureen Honey**, *Creating Rosie the Riveter* (University of Massachusetts Press, 1984). **Barry Lopez**, "A Voice," from *About This Life: Journeys on the Threshold of Memory* (New York: Alfred A. Knopf, 1998). **Paula Mathieu** and **Ken McAllister**, CRITT Web site (Critical Resources in Teaching with Technology), 1997. http://www.engl .uic.edu/~stp/. Reprinted by permission. **Ellen Metter**, *Facts in a Flash: A Research Guide for Writers* (Cincinnati, OH: Writer's Digest Books, 1999). **H. Moody**, "Grammar Terms— Invention of the Devil?" http://www.swcp.com/info/essays/ grammerterms.htm. **Phil Patton**, "How a Ridiculous Idea Mutated into a Marketing Star," *Smithsonian,* 1992. *Publication Manual of the American Psychological Association* (5th ed., Washington, DC: American Psychological Association, 2001), p. xxiii. **Leo Reisberg**, "Colleges Step-Up Efforts to Combat Alcohol Abuse," *The Chronicle of Higher Education,* June 12, 1998, Vol. 44 No. 40. **Avi Sadeh, Amiram Raviv**, and **Reut Gruber**, "Sleep Patterns and Sleep Disruptions in School-Age Children," *Developmental Psychology*, Vol. 36, No. 3, May 2000. **Jay Sankey**, From *Zen and the Art of Stand-Up Comedy.* Copyright © 1998. Reproduced by permission of Taylor & Francis / Routledge, Inc. http://www.routledge-ny.com. **Juliet B. Schor**, *The Overworked American* (New York: HarperCollins, 1998). **Sir Philip Sidney**, "His Lady's Cruelty," *The Oxford Book of English Verse 1250–1918* (London: Oxford University Press, 1973). **Nancy M. Smith** and **Ann D. Wallace**, "Plain English at a Glance," Plain English Network: The Business of Government in the Language of the People, http://www.plainlanguage.gov/library/ataglanc.htm. **Larry A. Tucker**, "Effect of Weight Training on Self-Concept: A Profile of Those Influenced Most," *Research Quarterly for Exercise and Sport*, 1983. **Mark Twain**, *Huckleberry Finn* (New York: HarperCollins, 1987). **The University of North Carolina**, Charlotte, "The Power of One," March, 1999. **Why milk.com**. Copyright © The National Milk Processor Promotion Board. Used with Permission. All rights reserved. http://www.whymilk.com/milku/diet_nutri_101 .html. **John Edgar Wideman**, *Brothers and Keepers* (New York: Random House, 1984). **Student Acknowledgments**: Summer Arrigo-Nelson, Jeanne Brown, Amy Burns, Kimlee Cunningham, Christine Reed-Davis, Robin Edwards, Jenifer Figliozzi, Tammy Jo Helton, Norrie Herrin, Kimberly Tullos.

edit

GLOSSARY OF USAGE AND TERMS

This glossary includes matters of usage (words that writers often find confusing or difficult, such as *farther* and *further*), grammatical terms (such as *verb*), and rhetorical terms (such as *indirect quotation*).

a, an Use *an* before a vowel (*an old film*) or silent *h* (*an honor*) and *a* before a consonant (*a classic, a hero*). (See 220-R.)

accept, except *Accept* means "to take or receive"; *except* means "excluding."

> Everyone **accepted** the invitation **except** Larry.

active voice (See **voice**.)

adverse, averse Someone opposed to something is *averse* to it; *adverse* conditions oppose achieving a goal.

advice, advise *Advice*, a noun, means "counsel" or "recommendations." *Advise*, a verb, means "to counsel or recommend."

> He tried to **advise** students who wanted no **advice**.

gloss

affect, effect The verb *affect* means "to influence." *Effect* as a noun means "a result" and, rarely, as a verb means "to cause something to happen."

> Because CFCs may **affect** the ozone layer with an uncertain **effect** on global warming, our goal is to **effect** changes in public attitudes.

aggravate, irritate *Aggravate* means "to worsen"; *irritate* means "to bother."

ain't Replace *ain't* in formal writing with *am not*, *is not*, or *are not*. The contractions *aren't* and *isn't* are more acceptable but are still informal.

all ready, already *All ready* means "prepared"; *already* means "by that time."

> Sam was **all ready**, but the team had **already** gone.

all right Always spell this as two words, not as *alright*.

all together, altogether Use *all together* to mean "everyone"; use *altogether* to mean "completely."

We were **all together** on our plan, but it was **altogether** too much to organize by Friday.

allude, elude *Allude* means "refer indirectly"; *elude* means "escape."

allusion, illusion An *allusion* is a reference to something; an *illusion* is a vision or false belief.

a lot Even when spelled correctly as two words, not as *alot*, *a lot* may be too informal for some writing. Use *many* or *much* instead.

a.m., p.m. These abbreviations may be capitals or lowercase (see 34a).

among, between Use *between* when something involves two things; use *among* for three or more.

The fight **between** the two players led to a debate **among** the umpire and the managers.

amount, number *Amount* refers to a quantity of something that can't be divided into separate units; *number* refers to countable objects.

The recipe uses a **number** of spices and a small **amount** of milk.

an (See **a, an**.)
analytical synthesis (See **synthesis**.)
and etc. (See **etc**.)
and/or Because *and/or* is imprecise, choose one of the words, or revise.
ante-, anti- The prefix *ante-* means "before" or "predating," while *anti-* means "against" or "opposed."
antecedent The noun or pronoun to which another word (usually a pronoun) refers (see 18c).
anyone, any one *Anyone* is an indefinite pronoun; you may also use *any* to modify *one*, in the sense of "any individual thing or person."

Anyone can dive, but the coach has little time for **any one** person.

anyplace Replace this term in formal writing with *anywhere*, or revise.
anyways, anywheres Avoid these versions of *anyway* and *anywhere*.
appositive A noun or pronoun that renames or stands for a prior noun.

gloss

appositive phrase An **appositive** (usually a noun) and its modifiers that rename or stand for a prior noun to add detail to a sentence.

Ken and Beth, **my classmates**, won an award.

as, like Used as a preposition, *as* indicates a precise comparison. *Like* indicates a resemblance or similarity.

Remembered **as** a man of habit, Kant, **like** many other philosophers, was thoughtful and intense.

as to *As to* is considered informal in many contexts.

| INFORMAL | The media speculated **as to** the film's success. |
| EDITED | The media speculated **about** the film's success. |

assure, ensure, insure Use *assure* to imply a promise, *ensure* to imply a certain outcome, and *insure* to imply something legal or financial.

The surgeon **assured** the pianist that his hands would heal by May. To **ensure** that, the musician **insured** his hands with Lloyd's of London.

at In writing, drop *at* in direct and indirect questions.

| SPOKEN | Jones asked where his attorney was **at**. |
| EDITED | Jones asked where his attorney **was.** |

gloss

awful, awfully Use *awful* (adjective) to modify a noun; use *awfully* (adverb) to modify a verb.

He played **awfully** on that hole and sent an **awful** shot into the pond.

awhile, a while *Awhile* (one word) acts as an adverb; it is not preceded by a preposition. *A while* acts as a noun (with the article *a*) and is used in prepositional phrases.

The homeless family stayed **awhile** at the shelter because the children had not eaten for **a while**.

bad, badly Use *bad* (adjective) with a noun or linking verb expressing feelings, not the adverb *badly* (see 19f).

because, since Use *since* to indicate time, not causality in place of the more formal and precise *because*.

being as, being that Write *because* instead.

beside, besides Use *beside* to mean "next to." Use *besides* for "also" (adverb) or "except" (adjective).

>**Besides** being the firm's tax specialist, Klein would review nearly any document placed **beside** him.

better, had better Revise to *ought to* or *should* in formal writing.

between (See **among, between.**)

block quotation A quotation long enough to require separating it from the text in an indented block (see 10b).

bring, take *Bring* implies movement from somewhere else to close at hand; *take* implies the opposite direction.

>**Bring** more coffee, but **take** away the muffins.

broke *Broke* is the past tense of *break*, not the past participle (see 19a).

DRAFT	The computer was **broke**.
EDITED	The computer was **broken.**

burst, bursted *Burst* implies an outward explosion: The boys *burst* the balloon. Do not use *bursted* for the past tense.

bust, busted Avoid *bust* or *busted* to mean "broke."

COLLOQUIAL	The van **bust** down on the trip.
EDITED	The van **broke** down on the trip.

but however, but yet Choose one word of each pair.

can, may *Can* implies ability; *may* implies permission or uncertainty.

>Bart **can** drive, but his dad **may** not lend him the car.

can't hardly, can't scarcely Use these positively (*can hardly, can scarcely*), or simply use *can't* (see 19f).

capital, capitol *Capital* refers to a government center, a letter, or money; *capitol* refers to a government building.

censor, censure *Censor* means the act of shielding something from the public, such as a book. *Censure* implies punishment or critical labeling.

center around Use *center on*, *focus on*, or *revolve around*.

choose, chose Use *choose* for the present and *chose* for the past tense.
cite, site *Cite* means to acknowledge someone's work; *site* means a place.

> Phil **cited** field studies of the Anasazi **site**.

clause A word group with a subject and a verb. A **main** (independent) clause can stand on its own; a **subordinate** (dependent) clause begins with a subordinating word (*because, although, which, that*) and cannot stand alone (see 25b).

> **Because he lost his balance**, Sam fell on the ice.

climactic, climatic *Climactic* refers to the culmination of something; *climatic* refers to weather conditions.
comma splice Two or more sentences (main clauses) incorrectly joined with a comma. (See Chapter 16.)
comparative The form of an adjective or adverb showing that the word it modifies is compared to one other thing (see 223-R). The comparative form adds *-er* or *more* (*faster, more adept*). (See **superlative**.)
compare to, compare with Use *compare to* and *liken to* for similarities between two things. Use *compare with* for both similarities and differences.

> **Compared with** the boy's last illness, this virus, which the doctor **compared to** a tiny army, was mild.

complement A word (noun, pronoun, adjective) or phrase tied to a subject by a **linking verb** (*becomes, is, seems*). A **subject complement** describes or renames a subject: Nan seems **tired**. An **object complement** does the same for a direct object: Brad ate the pizza **cold**. (See 211-R.)
complement, compliment *Complement* means "an accompaniment"; *compliment* means "words of praise."

> The guests **complimented** the chef on the menu, which **complemented** the event perfectly.

compound modifier Two or more words that work as a single modifier (**wood-burning** fireplace).
compound object Two or more objects joined by *and* or *both . . . and*.
compound subject Two or more subjects joined by *and* or *both . . . and*.

compound word A word made up of two or more independent words (such as *superman* or *father-in-law*).

conjunction A word that joins two elements in a sentence. **Coordinating conjunctions** (*and, but, or, nor, for, yet, so*) link grammatically equal elements—compound subjects, verbs, objects, and modifiers. **Subordinating conjunctions** (*because, although, while, if*) create a subordinate clause. (See Chapter 25.)

conjunctive adverb An adverb (*however, moreover, therefore*) that joins sentences or sentence elements, showing how they are related (see 25a).

continual, continuous *Continual* implies that something recurs; *continuous* implies that it is constant or unceasing.

The **continual** noise of the jets was less annoying than the traffic **continuously** circling the airport.

coordinate adjectives Two adjectives, each modifying a noun on its own, separated by a comma. If the first modifies the second (which modifies the noun), they are **noncoordinate adjectives**, not separated by a comma.

coordinating conjunction One of seven words (*and, but, or, nor, for, yet, so*) that link equal elements (see 25a). (See **conjunction**.)

coordination A sentence structure using **coordinating conjunctions** to link and weight main clauses equally (see 25a, c).

could of, would of Replace these, often pronounced as they are misspelled, with *could have* or *would have*.

couple, couple of In formal writing, use *a few* or *two*.

criteria *Criteria* is the plural form of *criterion*.

PLURAL   The **criteria** were too strict to follow.

critical synthesis (See **synthesis**.)

curriculum *Curriculum* is the singular form. For the plural, use either *curricula* or *curriculums* consistently.

dangling modifier (See **misplaced modifier**.)

data Widely used for both singular and plural, *data* technically is plural; *datum* refers to a single piece of data. If in doubt, use the plural.

PLURAL   These **data** are not very revealing.

gloss

different from, different than Use *different from* when an object follows; use *different than* (not *from what*) when a clause follows.

> Jim's tacos are **different from** Lena's; his enchiladas now are **different than** they were when he began to cook.

direct quotation A statement that repeats someone's exact words, set off by quotation marks (see 10b). (See also **indirect quotation**.)

discreet, discrete *Discreet* means "reserved or cautious"; *discrete* means "distinctive" or "explicit."

disinterested, uninterested *Disinterested* implies impartiality or objectivity; *uninterested* implies lack of interest.

disruptive modifier (See **misplaced modifier**.)

done *Done* is a past participle, not past tense (see 19a).

| DRAFT | The runner **done** her best at the meet. |
| EDITED | The runner **did** her best at the meet. |

don't, doesn't Contractions may be too informal in some contexts. Ask your reader, or err on the side of formality (*do not, does not*).

double negative Avoid double negatives (see 19f).

DRAFT	The state **hasn't** done **nothing** about it.
EDITED	The state **has** done **nothing** about it.
EDITED	The state **hasn't** done **anything** about it.

due to To mean "because," use *due to* only after a form of the verb *be*. Avoid the wordy *due to the fact that*.

DRAFT	The mayor collapsed **due to** fatigue.
EDITED	The mayor's collapse was **due to** fatigue.
EDITED	The mayor collapsed **because** of fatigue.

effect, affect (See **affect, effect**.)

e.g. Avoid this abbreviation meaning "for example."

| AWKWARD | Her positions on issues, **e.g.**, gun control, are very liberal. |
| EDITED | Her positions on issues **such as** gun control are very liberal. |

gloss

ellipsis A series of three spaced periods showing a reader where something has been left out of a quotation (see 38d).

emigrate from, immigrate to People *emigrate from* one country and *immigrate to* another. *Migrate* implies moving about (*migrant workers*) or settling temporarily.

ensure (See **assure, ensure, insure**.)

enthused Avoid *enthused* for *enthusiastic* in writing.

especially, specially *Especially* implies "in particular"; *specially* means "for a specific purpose."

It was **especially** important to follow the **specially** designed workouts.

etc. Avoid this abbreviation in formal writing; supply a complete list, or use a phrase like *so forth*.

INFORMAL   The march was a disaster: it rained, the protesters had no food, **etc.**

EDITED   The march was a disaster: the protesters were wet and hungry.

eventually, ultimately Use *eventually* to imply that an outcome follows a series (or lapse) of events; use *ultimately* to imply that a final act ends a series of events.

Eventually, the rescuers pulled the last victim from the wreck, and **ultimately** there were no casualties.

everyday, every day *Everyday* (adjective) modifies a noun. *Every day* is a noun (*day*) modified by *every*.

Every day in the Peace Corps, Monique faced the **everyday** task of boiling her drinking water.

everyone, every one *Everyone* is a pronoun; *every one* is an adjective followed by a noun.

Everyone was dazzled by **every one** of the desserts.

exam In formal writing, readers may prefer the full term, *examination*.

except (See **accept, except**.)

expletive construction Opening with *there is, there are*, or *it is* to delay the subject until later in the sentence (see 20b).

explicit, implicit *Explicit* means that something is openly stated, *implicit* that it is implied or suggested.

gloss

farther, further *Farther* implies a distance that can be measured; *further* implies one that cannot.

The **farther** they hiked, the **further** their friendship deteriorated.

faulty parallelism (See **parallelism**.)

faulty predication A sentence flaw in which the second part (the predicate) comments on a topic different from the one in the first part (see 21b).

FAULTY	The **presence** of ozone in smog is the **chemical** that causes eye irritation.
EDITED	The **ozone** in smog is the **chemical** that causes eye irritation.

female, male Use these terms only to call attention to gender specifically, as in a research report. Otherwise, use *man* or *woman* unless such usage is sexist (see 27b).

fewer, less Use *fewer* for things that can be counted, and use *less* for quantities that cannot be divided.

The new bill had **fewer** supporters and **less** media coverage.

first person Pronouns (*I*, *we*) for the person speaking. (See **person**.)

firstly Use *first*, *second*, *third* when enumerating points.

form The spelling or ending that shows a word's role in a sentence. (See Chapter 19.)

former, latter *Former* means "the one before" and *latter* means "the one after." The pair must refer to only two things.

fragment Part of a sentence incorrectly treated as complete. (See 15a–b.)

freshman, freshmen Readers may consider these terms sexist. Unless you are using an established term (such as the Freshman Colloquium), use *first-year student*.

fused sentence Two or more complete sentences incorrectly joined without any punctuation; also called a **run-on sentence**. (See Chapter 16.)

genre The form or type of text to which a work conforms (play, novel, lab report, essay, memo).

get Replace this word with more specific verbs.

INFORMAL	King's last speeches **got** nostalgic.
EDITED	King's last speeches **turned** nostalgic.

gloss

go, say Some speakers use *go* and *goes* very informally for *say* and *says*. Revise this usage in all writing.

gone, went Do not use *went* (the past tense of *go*) in place of the past participle form *gone*.

| DRAFT | The officers **should have went** to the captain. |
| EDITED | The officers **should have gone** to the captain. |

good and In formal writing, avoid this term to mean "very" (*good and* tired).

good, well *Good* (an adjective) means "favorable" (a *good* trip). *Well* (an adverb) means "done favorably." Avoid informal uses of *good* for *well*.

got to Avoid *got* or *got to* in place of *must* or *have to*.

| SPOKEN | I **got to** improve my grade in statistics. |
| WRITTEN | I **have to** improve my grade in statistics. |

great Formally, avoid *great* as an adjective meaning "wonderful"; use it to mean "large" or "monumental."

hanged, hung Some readers will expect you to use *hanged* exclusively to mean execution by hanging and *hung* to refer to anything else.

have, got (See **got to**.)

have, of (See **could of, would of**.)

he, she Avoid privileging male forms (see 27b).

helping verb A form of a verb such as *be*, *do*, or *have* that can be combined with a main verb (see 215-R).

hopefully Some readers may object when this word modifies an entire clause ("*Hopefully, her health will improve*"). When in doubt, use it only as "feeling hopeful."

however (See **but however, but yet**.)

hung (See **hanged, hung**.)

if, whether Use *if* before a specific outcome (stated or implied); use *whether* to consider alternatives.

If the technology can be perfected, we may soon have three-dimensional television. But **whether** we will be able to afford it is another question.

illogical comparison (See **incomplete sentence**.)

gloss

illusion (See **allusion, illusion**.)

immigrate to (See **emigrate from, immigrate to**.)

implicit (See **explicit, implicit**.)

incomplete comparison (See **incomplete sentence**.)

incomplete sentence A sentence that fails to complete an expected logical or grammatical pattern An **incomplete comparison** leaves out the element to which something is compared; an **illogical comparison** seems to compare things that cannot be reasonably compared. (See Chapter 21.)

independent clause (See **main clause**.)

indirect question A sentence whose main clause is a statement and whose embedded clause asks a question. Treat these as statements, not questions.

Phil wondered **what the study would show**.

indirect quotation A quotation in which a writer reports the substance of someone's words but not the exact words used. Quotation marks are not needed. (See **direct quotation**; see Chapter 31.)

in regard to Replace this wordy phrase with *about*.

inside of, outside of When you use *inside* or *outside* to mark locations, omit *of: Inside* the hut was a child.

insure (See **assure, ensure, insure**.)

interpolation Your own words, marked with brackets, introduced into a direct quotation from someone else (see 38c).

interrupter A parenthetical remark such as *in fact* or *more importantly*.

irregardless Avoid this erroneous form of *regardless*.

irritate (See **aggravate, irritate**.)

its, it's *Its* is a possessive pronoun; *it's* is a contraction for *it is*. (See Chapter 30.) Some readers object to contractions in formal writing.

-ize, -wise Some readers object to turning nouns or adjectives into verbs by adding *-ize* (*finalize, itemize, computerize*). Avoid adding *-wise* to words: "Weather-*wise*, it's chilly."

keyword A word in a database, catalog, or index used to identify a topic.

kind, sort, type Precede these singular nouns with *this*, not *these*. In general, use more precise words.

kind of, sort of Avoid these informal expressions (meaning "a little," "rather," or "somewhat") in academic and workplace writing.

gloss

latter (See **former, latter.**)

lay, lie *Lay* is a verb that needs a direct object (not the self). *Lie*, "place in a resting position," refers to the self; it takes the past tense form *lay* (see 19a).

less (See **fewer, less.**)

lie (See **lay, lie.**)

like (See **as, like.**)

limiting modifier A word such as *only*, *almost*, or *just* that qualifies a word, usually the one that follows it.

linking verb A verb that expresses a state of being or an occurrence: *is*, *seems*, *becomes*, *grows*.

literally In both factual and figurative (not true to fact) statements, avoid *literally*.

DRAFT	Jed **literally** died when he saw the hotel.
REDUNDANT	Jed **literally gasped** when he saw the hotel.
EDITED	Jed **gasped** when he saw the hotel.

loose, lose *Loose* (rhyming with *moose*) is an adjective meaning "not tight." *Lose* (rhyming with *snooze*) is a present tense verb meaning "to misplace."

lots (See **a lot.**)

main clause A word group with a subject and a verb that can stand on its own as a sentence. (See **clause.**)

may (See **can, may.**)

maybe, may be *Maybe* means *possibly*; *may be* is part of a verb structure.

The President **may be** speaking now, so **maybe** we should listen.

media, medium Technically plural, *media* is frequently used as a singular noun to refer to the press. *Medium* generally refers to a conduit or method of transmission.

The **media** is not covering the story accurately.

The telephone is a useful **medium** for planning.

might of (See **could of, would of.**)

mighty Omit or replace this with *very* in formal writing.

misplaced modifier A modifier incorrectly placed relative to the word it modifies (its headword). (See Chapter 22.)

gloss

mixed sentence A sentence with a mismatched or shifted grammatical structure. (See Chapter 21.)

modifier A word or word group, acting as an adjective or adverb, that qualifies the meaning of another word (see 19e–f).

modify The function of adjectives and adverbs that add to, qualify, limit, or extend the meaning of other words.

Ms. To avoid sexist labeling of women by marital status (not marked in men's titles), use *Ms.* unless you have reason to use *Miss* or *Mrs.* (as in the name of the character *Mrs. Dalloway*). Use professional titles when appropriate (*Dr.*, *Professor*, *Senator*, *Mayor*).

must of, must have (See **could of**, **would of**.)

nominalization A noun (*modernization*, *verbosity*) created from a verb (*modernize*) or adjective (*verbose*). (See 20b.)

noncoordinate adjectives (See **coordinate adjectives**.)

nonrestrictive modifier (See **restrictive modifier**.)

nor, or Use *nor* for negative and *or* for positive constructions.

NEGATIVE	Neither rain **nor** snow will slow the team.
POSITIVE	Either rain **or** snow may delay the game.

nothing like, nowhere near In formal writing, avoid these informal phrases used to compare two things.

noun string A sequence of nouns used to modify a main noun (*multifunction modulation control device*) that may seem abstract or technical to readers.

nowheres Use *nowhere* instead.

number The way of showing whether a noun or pronoun is **singular** (one) or **plural** (two or more). Subjects and verbs must agree in number as must pronouns and the nouns they modify. (See Chapter 18; see also **amount**, **number**.)

object The words in a sentence that tell who or what receives the action.

The class cleaned up **the park**.

of, have (See **could of**, **would of**.)

off of Use *off* instead.

gloss

OK When you write formally, use *OK* only in dialogue. If you mean "good" or "acceptable," use these terms.

on account of In formal writing, use *because*.

outside of (See **inside of, outside of**.)

parallelism The expression of similar or related ideas in similar grammatical form (see Chapter 24).

paraphrase To rewrite a passage in your own words, preserving the essence and detail of the original.

passive voice (See **voice**.)

per Use *per* to mean "by the," as in *per hour*, not "according to," as in *per your instructions*.

percent, percentage Use *percent* with numbers (*ten percent*); use *percentage* for a statistical part of something (*a large percentage of the budget*).

person The form that a noun or pronoun takes to identify the subject of a sentence. **First person** is someone speaking (*I, we*); **second person** is someone spoken to (*you*); **third person** is someone being spoken about (*he, she, it, they*). (See Chapter 18.)

personal pronoun A pronoun that designates persons or things, such as *I, me, you, him, we, you, they*. (See 221-R.)

phrase A word group without a subject, a verb, or both. (See **clause**.)

plagiarism The unethical or illegal practice of using another writer's words or text as your own without acknowledging their source (see 10d).

plus Replace *plus* with *and* to join two main clauses. Use *plus* only to mean "in addition to."

possessive A pronoun (*mine, hers, yours, theirs*) or noun (*the **bird's** egg*) that expresses ownership. (See 19c.)

precede, proceed *Precede* means "come before"; *proceed* means "go ahead."

predicate The words in a sentence that indicate an action, relationship, or condition—typically a **verb phrase** following the subject of the sentence. A **simple predicate** is a verb or verb phrase; to these, a **complete predicate** adds modifiers or other words that receive action or complete the verb.

prefix An addition, such as *un-* in *unforgiving*, at the beginning of a word. (See **suffix**.)

pretty Use *pretty* to mean "attractive," not "somewhat" or "rather" (as in *pretty good, pretty hungry*).

gloss

primary source Research material in or close to original form (see 8a).
principal, principle *Principal* is a noun meaning "an authority" or "head of a school" or an adjective meaning "leading" ("a *principal* objection to the testimony"). *Principle* is a noun meaning "belief or conviction."
proceed (See **precede, proceed**.)

quote, quotation Formally, *quote* is a verb, and *quotation* is a noun. Some readers object to *quote* as an abbreviation of *quotation*.

raise, rise *Raise* is a transitive verb meaning "to lift up." *Rise* is an intransitive verb (it takes no object) meaning "to get up or move up."

He **raised** his head to watch the sun **rise**.

rarely ever Use *rarely* alone, not paired with *ever*.
real, really Use *real* as an adjective; use *really* as an adverb (see 19f).
reason is because, reason is that Avoid these wordy phrases. (See 21b.)
redundancy The use of unnecessary or repeated words (see 26a).
reference chain A sequence of pronouns whose **antecedent**, the word to which they refer, is stated in the opening sentence of a passage (see 17b).
regarding (See **in regard to**.)
regardless (See **irregardless**.)
relative clause A clause that modifies a noun or pronoun and begins with a **relative pronoun** (*who, whom, whose, which, that*).

Jen found a Web site **that** had valuable links.

respectfully, respectively Use *respectfully* for "with respect" and *respectively* to imply an order or sequence.

The senate **respectfully** submitted revisions for items 4 and 10, **respectively**.

restrictive modifier A **restrictive modifier** supplies information essential to the meaning of a sentence and is added without commas. A **nonrestrictive modifier** adds useful or interesting information not essential to the meaning and set off by commas (see 28d).
rise (See **raise, rise**.)
run-on sentence (See **fused sentence**.)

gloss

says (See **go, says**.)

second person The pronoun (*you*) referring to the person spoken to. (See **person**.)

secondary source Research information that analyzes, interprets, or comments on primary sources (see 8a). (See also **primary source**.)

sentence A group of words with both a subject and a complete verb that can stand on its own. (See **fragment, comma splice, fused sentence**; see 15a and Chapter 16.)

sentence cluster A group of sentences that develop related ideas or information.

set, sit *Set* means "to place"; *sit* means "to place oneself" (see 19a).

should of (See **could of, would of**.)

shift An inappropriate switch in **person, number, mood, tense**, or **topic**. (See Chapter 23.)

since (See **because, since**.)

sit (See **set, sit**.)

site (See **cite, site**.)

so Some readers object to the use of *so* in place of *very*.

somebody, some body (See **anyone, any one**.)

someone, some one (See **anyone, any one**.)

sometime, some time, sometimes *Sometime* refers to a vague future time; *sometimes* means "every once in a while." *Some time* is an adjective (*some*) modifying a noun (*time*).

> **Sometime** every winter, **sometimes** after a project is finished, the crew takes **some time** off.

sort (See **kind, sort**.)

specially (See **especially, specially**.)

split infinitive An infinitive is the base form of a verb paired with *to* (*to run*). Some readers object to another word placed between the two (to **quickly** run). (See 22a.)

squinting modifier (See **misplaced modifier**.)

stationary, stationery *Stationary* means "standing still"; *stationery* refers to writing paper.

subject In a sentence, the doer or thing talked about, typically placed before a verb phrase. A **simple subject** consists of one or more nouns (or pronouns) naming the doer; to this a **complete subject** adds modifiers.

gloss

subject complement (See **complement**.)

subordinate clause A word group with a subject and a verb that is introduced by a subordinator (*because, although, that, which*). It must be connected to a main clause (which can stand alone). (See **clause**.)

subordinating conjunction A word (*because, although, while, if*) that introduces a subordinate clause, a word group with a subject and verb that cannot stand alone and must be connected to a main clause. (See **conjunction;** see 25b.)

such Some readers will expect *that* to follow *such*.

The team solved **such** a complex problem **that** everyone cheered.

suffix An addition, such as *-ly* in *quickly*, at the end of a word. (See **prefix**.)

summary A concise restatement in your own words, boiling a passage or source down to essentials (see 9a).

superlative The form of an adjective or adverb showing that the word it modifies is compared to two or more other things (see 223-R). The superlative adds *-est* or *most* (*fastest, most adept*). (See **comparative**.)

suppose to Use the correct form, *supposed to*, even though the *-d* is not always heard in pronunciation.

sure, surely Formally, use *sure* to mean "certain." Use *surely*, not *sure* as an adverb (see 19f).

He has **surely** studied hard and is **sure** to pass.

sure and, try and Write *sure to* and *try to* instead.

synthesis The distilling of separate elements into a single, unified entity. For a research paper, an **analytical synthesis** relates summaries of several sources while a **critical synthesis** presents conclusions about a variety of perspectives, opinions, or interpretations (see 9a–b).

take (See **bring, take**.)

tense The form a verb takes to indicate time—past, present, or future tense (see 213-R).

than, then *Than* is used to compare; *then* implies a sequence of events or a causal relationship.

Lil played harder **than** Eva; **then** the rain began.

gloss

that, which In formal writing, use *that* when a clause is essential to the meaning of a sentence (restrictive modifier) and *which* when it does not provide essential information (nonrestrictive modifier) (see 28d).

theirself, theirselves, themself Replace these with *themselves* to refer to more than one person and *himself* or *herself* to refer to one person.

them Avoid *them* as a subject or to modify a subject, as in "*Them* are fresh" or "*Them* apples are crisp." Replace with *they, these, those,* or *the* with a noun (*the apples*).

then (See **than, then**.)

there, their, they're These forms sound alike, but *there* shows location, *their* is a possessive pronoun, and *they're* contracts *they* and *are*.

Look over **there**. **Their** car ran out of gas. **They're** starting to walk.

third person Pronouns (*he, she, it, they*) that indicate the person or thing spoken about. (See **person**.)

thusly Replace this term with *thus* or *therefore*.

till, until, 'til Some readers will find *'til* and *till* informal; use *until*.

to, too, two These words sound alike, but *to* is a preposition showing direction, *too* means "also," and *two* is a number.

Ed went **to** the lake **two** times and took Han **too**.

toward, towards Prefer *toward* in formal writing.

transitional expression Expressions (*therefore, in addition*) that link one idea, sentence, or paragraph to the next, helping readers relate ideas.

try and, try to (See **sure and, try and**.)

ultimately (See **eventually, ultimately**.)

uninterested (See **disinterested, uninterested**.)

unique Use *unique*, not *most* or *more unique* (see 19g).

until (See **till, until, 'til**.)

use to, used to Write *used to*, even though the *-d* is not always clearly pronounced.

verb The word in a sentence that expresses action (*jump*), occurrence (*happen*), or state of being (*be*). (See 19a and 213-R–220-R.)

gloss

voice A verb is in the **active voice** when the doer of the action is the subject of the sentence and in the **passive voice** when the goal or object of the sentence is the subject. (See 216-R.)

ACTIVE   The company **paid** the claim.

PASSIVE   The claim **was paid** by the company.

wait for, wait on Use *wait on* for a clerk's or server's job; use *wait for* to mean "to await someone's arrival."

well (See **good, well**.)

went (See **gone, went**.)

were, we're *Were* is a verb; *we're* is a contraction for "we are."

where . . . at (See **at**.)

whether (See **if, whether**.)

which (See **that, which**.)

who, whom Though the distinction between these words is disappearing, many readers will expect you to use *whom* for an object. Err on the side of formality, or rewrite (see 19d).

who's, whose *Who's* is a contraction for "who is"; *whose* shows possession.

The programmer **who's** joining our division searched for the person **whose** bag he took by mistake.

-wise (See **-ize, -wise**.)

would of (See **could of, would of**.)

yet (See **but however, but yet**.)

your, you're *Your* is a possessive pronoun; *you're* contracts "you are."

If **you're** taking math, you'll need **your** calculator.

gloss

INDEX

Note: Page numbers ending in G refer to glossary entries; R to the Resources; and T to the Tips. *See* references identify appropriate or related index entries. Turn to the Glossary to find entries discussed only there.

index

index

QUICK TIPS FOR WRITERS, READERS, AND SPEAKERS

Tips for Academic Writers
Who are your academic readers?
- Are they classmates, your teacher, or others?
- What do your readers already know?
- What do they want to find out?
- What do they want you to demonstrate?

What do academic readers expect you to do?
- Analyze or interpret a text or an event.
- Review and cite related theory and research.
- Reason logically and critically about a question.
- Bring fresh insights, and draw your own conclusions.

What might you try to do in your writing?
- State your thesis and main points clearly.
- Use pertinent detail to support your views.
- Write clearly and logically, even on a complex topic.
- Acknowledge other views as you explore a topic.

What form should you use?
- Analyze the criteria explained in your assignment.
- Ask about the form of writing required; review examples of essays, arguments, reports, reviews, lab reports, or other required forms.
- Ask advice from other students; look over comments from peers or instructors on previous papers of the same type.

Taking It Online
- Reading and writing across the disciplines
  http://writing.colostate.edu/references/documents.cfm

Tips for Workplace Writers
Who are your workplace readers?
- Are they co-workers, supervisors, clients, customers, government agencies, work groups, or others?
- What do your readers already know?
- What do they expect you to provide?
- Do they need to decide, implement, or understand?

What might these readers expect you to do?
- Provide or request information.
- Analyze problems.
- Recommend actions or solutions.
- Identify and evaluate alternatives.

What might you try to do in your writing?
- Focus on the task, problem, or goal.
- Present the issue clearly and accurately.
- Organize efficiently, and summarize for busy readers.
- Use concise, clear, direct prose.

What form should you use?
- Ask your supervisor or colleagues what form of writing (or oral presentation) your audience expects.
- Review examples of memos, letters, charts, reports, manuals, evaluations, or other expected forms.
- Follow the approach and pattern generally used in this form and in models prepared at your workplace.

Taking It Online
- Résumés
  http://owl.english.purdue.edu/workshops/hypertext/ResumeW/index.html
  http://jobstar.org/tools/resume/
- *Plain Language Action Network*
  http://www.plainlanguage.gov/main.htm

Tips for Public Writers
Who are your readers?
- Are they members of your organization, possible supporters of your cause, public officials, community activists, local residents, or others?
- What do your readers value? What concerns them?
- What do readers want to accomplish?
- What do you have in common? Where do you differ?

What might these readers expect you to do?
- Provide issue-oriented information, especially local background, data, and evidence.
- Encourage civic involvement and decision making.
- Persuade others to support a cause or issue.

What might you try to do in your writing?
- Persuade, enlighten, alert, or energize readers to act.
- Recommend policies, actions, or solutions.
- Be an advocate for your cause.
- Present relevant evidence to support your position.
- Recognize the interests and goals of others.

What form should you use?
- Work collaboratively with others who have experience preparing flyers, newsletters, brochures, fact sheets, committee reports, public comments, letters, or other forms.
- Review similar materials prepared by your group or by other civic or special-interest groups.

Taking It Online
- Press releases
  http://www.stetson.edu/~rhansen/prguide.html
- Grant proposals
  http://www.hfsp.org/how/grantsmanship.htm
  http://fdncenter.org/learn/shortcourse/prop1.html

Tips for Readers
Preread before you read
- Review any abstract, table of contents, menu, or headings.
- Note the author's credentials, publication date, and similar information on the title or home page.
- Scan for unfamiliar key words and concepts.
- Turn to an introductory text or encyclopedia article for background or definitions of complex terms.
- Predict what you expect based on similar texts.

Respond as you read
- Pause and assess as you reach logical breaks.
- Note what you've learned and what's confusing.
- Skim each section after you have read it, reviewing major points and their connections.
- Summarize chunks, briefly noting a section's main point.
- Highlight or make notes during your second reading—not your first—so you know what's really important.
- Share insights with classmates or work colleagues, comparing reactions to content and language.

Follow up after you read
- Write your interpretations, questions, objections, evaluations, or applications (to class, work, service learning, or civic activities) in the margins if the text is yours.
- Respond in a journal or on note cards, noting what you think and what the author says.
- Reread difficult material, skimming to trace its logic and studying or reading aloud key passages.

Taking It Online
- Evaluating reading
  http://www2.widener.edu/Wolfgram-Memorial-Library/webevaluation/examples.htm

Tips for Speakers
Plan ahead
- Review criteria for an academic assignment.
- Identify audience expectations and time limits.
- Gather accurate, persuasive resources.
- Group your information, or outline your remarks.
- Write out "talking points"—main points, transitions, key sentences, and reminders to yourself.
- Prepare visuals—and backups—so they are clear, large enough to read, and relevant to your talk.
- Prepare any handouts to supplement your talk.

Rehearse
- Practice aloud, and time your presentation.
- Ask others for suggestions on content or delivery.
- Practice more if you stumble, lose your place, or forget key ideas; refine your talking points.
- Try videotaping or tape recording to spot problems or distracting habits.
- Reprint or recopy your notes on cards that are easy to read and handle; number them in order.
- Practice with your visuals—and your backups.

Present
- Take a deep breath, speak slowly, and make eye contact with your audience. Don't apologize.
- Use your notes to recall your talk, not to read.
- Concentrate on your audience—not yourself, your visuals, your notes, or outside distractions.
- Refer to, but don't read, visuals and handouts.
- Field questions confidently and directly.

Taking It Online
- Speaking
  http://departments.mwc.edu/spkc/www/handouts.htm
  http://www.toastmasters.org/tips.asp

Tips for Collaborative Writers
Draft collaboratively
- Organize parallel drafting, dividing up the project so that each person drafts a particular section.
- Try team drafting, assigning two writers for each section so one picks up when another gets stuck.
- Consider intensive drafting with a close friend or colleague, both working undisturbed and exchanging drafts or one talking as the other types.
- Exchange drafts as your group revises, but appoint one person as editor to integrate final drafts.

Revise collaboratively
- Share your purpose and concerns with readers.
- Minimize apologies; everyone feels anxious about sharing a draft.
- Tape record responses, meet to discuss or take notes on comments, email, or annotate drafts.
- Recirculate a collaborative draft, or meet to revise.

Edit collaboratively
- Revise first; prepare a clean draft for peer editors.
- Alert peer readers to concerns or recurring problems.
- Use familiar labels and symbols when you read drafts.
- Make clear, specific comments.
- Note possible errors, but let the writer make repairs.
- Look for patterns, repeating the same errors.

Taking It Online
- "Online Technical Writing: Strategies for Peer-Reviewing and Team-Writing"
  http://www.io.com/~hcexres/tcm1603/acchtml/team.html
- "Prof. David's Guidelines for Collaborative Writing"
  http://www.uncp.edu/home/vanderhoof/syllabus/colab-rt.html

Tips for Online Writers

Who are your readers?
- Are they members of an online course conference, email correspondents, members of an electronic mailing list, participants in a newsgroup or Web forum, or random visitors to your Web site?
- What will readers expect of your course exchanges, messages, home page, or Web site?

What might these readers expect you to do?
- Follow netiquette, and adapt to group norms.
- Respect readers' time, interests, and privacy.
- Behave ethically online.

What might you try to do in your writing?
- Consider what readers will expect, want, or need to find as they follow a thread or access your Web site.
- Focus briefly on essentials in each screen or message.
- Supply reliable information based on your expertise.
- Provide attachments, graphics, and other materials so that readers can easily access (or skip) them.
- Relate screens, supply options, and update so that your Web site remains current and easy to navigate.
- Identify and update useful links.
- Include email information so readers can respond.

What form should you use?
- Lurk to observe expectations for messages and replies to conferences, mailing lists, or other groups.
- Follow course or workplace directions for attaching documents, graphics, or audio files.
- Analyze sample home pages and Web sites for ideas about design, navigation, and organization.

Taking It Online
- Netiquette
  http://www.fau.edu/netiquette/net/

Tips for Online Researchers

Find resources online

- Identify keywords related to your research questions.
- Try several search engines, especially those recommended by others.
- Use advanced search strategies.
- Follow links as you hunt for relevant sources.
- Print out or bookmark authoritative sites, pages, or links.

Screen sources as you search

- Be selective but flexible while you search.
- Measure sources against your research questions.
- Skip questionable sources that readers won't accept.
- Stay focused despite engaging—but irrelevant—links.
- Gather varied but reliable sources.
- Evaluate your search results as you work, and get expert advice from a librarian if needed.

Evaluate potentially useful sources

- Assess the interests, possible motives, and reputation of the author, sponsor, or online publisher.
- Determine whether the source is current, well edited, and straightforward about its viewpoint.
- Check for logic, claims, and supporting evidence.
- Compare information across sources to verify accuracy, fairness, and consistency.
- Assess the relevance and reliability of information as your academic, work, or public readers will.

Taking It Online

- *The Good, the Bad, and the Ugly*
  http://lib.nmsu.edu/instruction/eval.html
- "Evaluation of Information Sources"
  http://www.vuw.ac.nz/~agsmith/evaln/evaln.htm.

READ, RECOGNIZE, AND REVISE TEN SERIOUS ERRORS

These ten errors are identified in our research as among those most likely to confuse or irritate readers in the academic community. Whether errors distort meaning or suggest carelessness, they can distract readers from what you want to say and diminish the success of your writing.

1. The heavy rain turned the parking lot area to mud. **And stranded thousands of cars.**

   Fragment: 15

2. The promoters called **the insurance company they discovered** their coverage for accidents was limited.

   Fused Sentence: 16

3. After talking with the groundskeeper, the security chief said **he** would not be responsible for the safety of the crowd.

   Unclear Pronoun Reference: 17

4. The local authorities **hadn't scarcely** enough resources to cope with the flooding.

   Double Negative: 19f

5. **After announcing the cancellation from the stage, the crowd** began complaining to the promoters.

   Dangling Modifier: 22

6. Even the **promoters promise** to reschedule and honor tickets did little to stop the **crowds complaints.**

   Missing Possessive Apostrophe: 30

7. "The grounds are **slippery, the** mayor announced, "so please leave in an orderly manner."

   Missing Quotation Marks: 31

8. Away from the microphone, the mayor said, "I hope the security chief or the promoters **has** a plan to help everyone leave safely."

   Lack of Subject-Verb Agreement: 18

9. If **people** left the amphitheater quickly, **you** could get to **your** car without standing long in the rain.

   Shift: 23

10. **Although,** the muddy parking area caused problems, all the cars and **people, left** the grounds without incident.

    Unnecessary Commas: 28

Contents